THE MOM'S GUIDE TO
SURVIVING
WEST POINT

Lisa Browne Joiner *and* Deborah L. W. Roszel

you can do this — you're a. West Point Mom!

I love, Debbie

Lisa Browne Joiner and Deborah L. W. Roszel
www.momsguidetosurviving.com
Printed in the United States of America
Published by Light Messages Publishing
Durham, North Carolina
ISBN: 978-1-61153-030-8

It is said that to have a child is to forever have your heart walking around outside your body. To the three parts of my heart: Stephen, Matt, and Scott.
–LBJ

To Robert Mason Roszel:
Thank you for making me a West Point Mom.
–DLWR

CONTENTS

ACKNOWLEDGMENTS

In 2008, Debbie and I became West Point Moms. Our sons had received and accepted appointments to the most prestigious school in the country (in our opinion). What we didn't know then was how their college choice would impact our lives as moms. This experience was new mom territory for both of us.

Fortunately, we had the leadership of the moms of the West Point Parents' Club of Georgia. While so many of those moms helped us figure out the early months of our West Point experience, we'd especially like to thank Angelé Propst, who took us under her wing and was always there to answer questions and give moral support. Thanks also to Mary Ivey, who made it a special point to help Debbie find her way as a shy new club member, even giving Debbie her first West Point Mom T-shirt.

Debra Dalton, the West Point Parent Liaison (and Command Sergeant Mother), has been available pretty much 24/7 to help any West Point Mom in need. Her ideas and suggestions have been invaluable.

We are very thankful for our husbands, Steve Joiner and Rich Roszel. When we told them we wanted to help other West Point Moms by writing a book, they stepped up with not only loads of encouragement, but also the extra help necessary to free us up to write. We also want to thank them for their great ideas and suggestions—even the ones we didn't take. We appreciate their attention to detail. We like, too, that they laughed in the right places when they read our manuscript.

A special thanks to Elizabeth Roszel, who at eight years old is always eager to help. She read many pages of manuscript aloud to Debbie as they combined multiple versions of the manuscript into one polished final copy.

Matt Joiner was so patient in explaining everyday West Point events in terms even his mom could understand. Thanks, buddy!

There is no way we could have written this book without the aid of moms who had West Point experiences that we didn't have. Thank you to our contributing moms: Mary Ables, Cindy Winter-Hartley, Kris Wright, Amy Dawson, Anne Curry, Pam VanOteghem, and Manuella Pop. Many moms contributed in the chapters titled "Life Lessons," and "People Say the Darnedest Things." These quotes are from some of the over 1000 moms who make up the Facebook group West Point Moms. (Please join us if you're not there.)

Some other nice folks at West Point helped us in various ways. USMA Chaplain (COL) Mike Durham made sure the information in the chapter on religious expression was correct. The West Point AOG office helped us clarify the chapter titled "Support Your Local Academy." A special thank-you goes to CPT Emily Zukauskas, Office of the Staff Judge Advocate, who worked with us concerning trademark issues.

In addition to our husbands, several other gracious people

reviewed our manuscript and made gently critical suggestions for improvement. These included Kathy Brake, Linda Smigen, Maria Bailey, Kathleen Haley and Ronald A. Cook.

We would like to thank Betty Turnbull at Light Messages Publishing for her support and encouragement—and especially for the e-mail that arrived one day stating, "We would like to be your publisher." We so appreciate Elizabeth Turnbull for her assistance and patience in the editing process.

A very special thanks to two long-time and very talented friends: Jeff Rease and Bruce MacPherson. Jeff did the cover design and layout, along with the photography on the back. You can see his work at www.jeffrease.com. Bruce designed the cover illustration of the West Point Mom. Bruce can be contacted at brucemacdesign@gmail.com.

To our other kids: we promise that we love you all the same. You have given us plenty of fodder for a book; maybe the next one will be about you!

–LBJ, May 2012

FOREWORD

In the summer of 2008, my middle son left for West Point. I discovered that pictures of cadets were being posted on Facebook, and to view them I had to join. A few months later I wondered if any other West Point moms might want to share information about our experiences, so I created a Facebook group called West Point Moms. It turns out that many, many moms want a place to ask questions, brag, complain, and make friends. The group has grown to over 1000 moms. It's not an official information site from West Point, but we help each other with information moms want to know for all things West Point.

Over the next few years on West Point Moms, the same kinds of questions kept coming up. For example, in the spring, new Cadet Candidate moms asked about buying boots. In the winter, moms asked about what to wear to Plebe Parent Weekend. I thought, "Someone ought to write this stuff down." This book grew out of that desire to support other moms as we live through our cadets' West Point experiences. I mentioned the idea of a book to another West Point mom, my friend Debbie Roszel, and she was intrigued. We soon got together and laid out the plans for this book.

Debbie and I want you, our reader, to feel like you're having a chat over coffee with a girlfriend about what the

West Point experience is like. Of course, everyone's experience is going to be unique, but there are many commonalities. Our book is casual and conversational; we've tried to write in an informal way, speaking as we would to a new acquaintance with questions about having a son or daughter at West Point. We hope it will be helpful, and we further hope it will be as much fun to read as it has been to write.

A few notes are in order. First of all, regarding gender references: we both have sons at West Point, but we are quite aware that there are daughters there as well. In writing, we have made extensive efforts to be gender-neutral in all references to cadets, but sometimes it wasn't possible; please forgive us in advance.

As in a friendly visit, our discussions here are honest and open, but past experience is not always an indicator of future performance. Our experience at West Point may not be just like yours, as events and regulations change over time. We have checked and double-checked and triple-checked our facts, but this is not a definitive Department of Defense Directive on Parental Survival of the United States Military Academy. We try to direct you to official sources of information when appropriate.

Official language is abundant at West Point, and it is not always easy to understand from context clues alone—especially when abbreviations and acronyms are used, as they often are in the military. We've included a chapter called "Lingo" at the end of the book with definitions for a whole slew of West Point terms. We placed it at the end, rather than the beginning, so you can use it for reference as you would a glossary.

In a further effort to give you helpful information, we have included names of businesses and vendors both on post and in the local area of Highland Falls, but this book is not an endorsement of any of them, nor is it a slight to any we have omitted.

Our goal is to give you enough information to help you support your son or daughter and to help you remember that the main focus should really be the cadet's experience, not yours. Some moms have called these 47 months a roller coaster. So hang on, Mom... it's going to be a wild ride!

–LBJ, May 2012

INTRODUCTION

When my firstborn child left for college, I was bombarded with questions from friends: "Aren't you so sad? How can you stand it? Oh! The quiet! Do you just cry??" Not so much—the kid was just 45 miles up the street—not a big deal! He had just returned from a year as an exchange student. Forty-five miles vs. 6,000 miles: no-brainer! If I needed to see him, I'd get in the car. Number two son is at West Point, and it isn't 45 miles up the street from me. In fact, it's precisely 845 miles.

West Point isn't like a traditional college. Unless your friends have kids at service academies, they will not understand this. Your child has, in fact, joined the United States Army, is an active duty member whose status is "non-deployable student," and is assigned to a post called West Point for a 47-month educational training program.

Your friends will not "get" this. They can hop in the car, go visit their kids, take them to dinner... you cannot. They can call their kids whenever they want; you cannot. They can have their kids come visit at any time; you cannot. But what can you do? You can be proud—you can embrace that your child has chosen to become a member of the Long Gray Line—the oldest—the first service academy in America. My dad recently said, "West Point isn't like other schools."

Finally, he gets it.

The myriad emotions you are feeling are not the same ones your friends with kids at State U are feeling, but there is a large group of people who do understand: The West Point Moms. All over the country (and across the world, too) is a group of moms who have gone this way before you. When no one else understands what you are going through and how you feel, you can always reach out to your fellow West Point moms. We are in your West Point Parents' Clubs, online, and now in this book. By supporting each other, we are better equipped to support our cadets on their West Point journey. I'm glad you found the West Point Moms; we're here to help.

CHAPTER 1

Today I Walked a 10K
(an analogy for the journey so far)

I walked my first 10K for a good cause: fallen heroes. One of my heroes ran that 10K: my cadet son. As I walked alone at the back of the pack, he was very near the front. With all that time and no interruptions, I had plenty of opportunity to reflect. After overcoming the mental challenge to keep going and making the commitment to finish, I began to see parallels between this new adventure I was having and the 47-month adventure my son was experiencing. His adventure had really begun years earlier, when he was in sixth grade. I realized that his commitment had paralleled a lot of commitment and dedication on my part as well, and for possibly the first time I saw myself as a very special person—a West Point Mom.

Ten kilometers. I can do this. I can walk that far.

Excited and eager, my companions want to run. I start with them, but it is not my pace. I am not a runner; I am a walker. In walking, I find joy; in running, I find discomfort. Occasionally I run for sheer happiness, but it is not a steady, paced run like one needs in a 10K. Also, I can hardly run around in circles pretending to be an airplane here in the middle of several hundred people trying to get up a hill.

So I work my way to the edge of the pavement and begin my walk. It starts very slowly, because of the cause the runners are supporting. The race is to raise money for the families of fallen warriors, and posted along the route are signs with the names, hometowns, ages, and dates of death for one hundred ninety-one Soldiers (from Georgia) who have died in combat since 2001. How can I run past these names, these reminders of ultimate sacrifice? Only by the greatest exertion can I keep from falling to my knees in prayer, in sorrow and gratitude; I force myself to walk, moving slowly past the markers to the first turn.

Uncertain whether I should keep going or turn back, I keep my feet moving while I think about it. As a mom, I've often suggested activities for my children that, for various reasons, I can't fully participate in. I'm quite used to staying back and waiting for them to finish, and I really don't mind. I get some quiet time alone, or get a chance to meet someone new, or get a nap in the car. It is part of what I do, part of who I am. My oldest child is in this race, running near the front, and he'll be back so long before I will. I don't want him to have to wait for me.

I keep walking. I take off my race number, in case I decide not to keep on going.

But is there any reason why he can't wait for me? He's a grown man now, and he knew when we signed up that he'd finish before I would. I told him I'd not be running much, if at all. What if I just do this, as I set out to do, and let everyone do what they set out to do, and let any upset feelings get dealt with later? What if no one's even upset? What if I just think for myself, and not for everyone else, and stop trying to make the world better by bowing out of it? Hmm?

Hmm. I can do this. I can walk that far.

I adjust my baggage. Yes, I am a mom. My son didn't want to run with his race tee, so I offered to carry it for him, since I'd be moving at a slower pace. Now I have two race tees, a water bottle, and an American flag in my arms. I'm accustomed to this way of being. I'm the helper, the accommodator. I do what's needed to be sure the others in my party succeed. I carry; I hold; I pack; I plan. They fly. So on this day, when I want to have a go at flying, I am still a mom. It even says so on my T-shirt: "West Point Mom."

I am a mom in my choice of clothing as well. At the front of the pack are long, lean legs in short running shorts, muscular arms in sleeveless tops, athletic forms in form-fitting running gear. Here am I in my capri-length comfortable pants and a slightly oversized T-shirt. The pants are black since we're told that's slimming. And I am walking, just walking, pretty sure I'm not going to run at all.

And I am happy, happy just to be here. What a beautiful morning! The air is fresh, the breeze is pleasant, the lake is blue and calm. The birds are singing everywhere. Oh, and I can still hear the bagpiper playing the final strains of "Amazing Grace" from the start of the race, where he stands on the hill with all the names.

I have now been passed by two young mothers running behind strollers. I imagine I'm at the end of the line. I didn't look at a map of our route, but I wonder if it loops back toward the start. Perhaps if I'm really this slow, I should just turn in there and meet up with my party then, as they will likely be finishing at about that time.

There's that word again, "should." I have done what

I should do for so long. For the most part it's not been a problem for me, but I've created quite a few unnecessary "shoulds." I'm thinking this is one of them.

I hear a woman's voice behind me say, "I'm going as fast as I can go." I glance back over my shoulder and see a couple walking behind me. So, perhaps I'll have company on this trip after all. As they get closer, though, I realize they both have iPods, so conversation is not going to be a priority. I wonder why, if they're walking together, they'd want to have iPods. I just don't get that.

Mile 1. Well, that's something, then. I can do this. I can walk that far.

And the man behind me says to his wife, "A fifteen-minute mile. That's a good pace." I feel a little surge of satisfaction. A fifteen-minute mile was my goal. I guess I'm pretty good at pacing myself. That's really pleasing to me. I am getting to know myself in so many ways, and here is another. I've walked at about a fifteen-minute pace for most of my walks around home, but I hadn't consciously worked toward that here. So many things were going through my mind; it's just so reassuring that my body knew what to do, to set its own pace, to find its comfortable operating level, to achieve the desired goal. Pacing. I can definitely do this.

When the second mile marker appears, I have been walking for exactly thirty minutes. This is great. I'm not even thinking about it, just walking along at a steady quick pace, one foot and then the other.

Between Miles 2 and 3 I see my son, who has made the turn and is headed back toward the start. We greet one another. He's doing very well, running steadily at about tenth place. A little farther along I see my other "running partners," more than a mile ahead of me. I call to them that I'll be done at 10:00.

I realize I've decided, then. I am going to finish this. At a fifteen-minute pace, which is what I'd planned on, I can finish by 10:00, which I'd also hoped for. I think of how many trips I've taken, to New York or to Oklahoma, for visits at my sons' colleges; how I set a time that I want to arrive there, and then pace myself to achieve the goal. And I usually arrive almost exactly when I plan to arrive. Pacing.

I can do this. I can walk that far.

As I continue, I think of parallels between this walk and being a parent. Pacing is important in parenting, too. We have to do so many things as parents, and sometimes it seems we have to do them all at once. Sometimes it seems as if we can't keep going, but if we keep steady on the course, keep doing the little things one after another, we can accomplish much. Pacing.

I didn't get to be a West Point Mom by giving up early, or by taking shortcuts. I am a West Point Mom because I kept going, kept my steps steady, and made sure my son was following along. A West Point Mom! What an accomplishment!

As the steps continue, I begin to think about the school years leading to West Point. I've passed the three-mile mark now, about halfway through. In a school career, that would be like finishing sixth grade. That was a challenging year. I'm heading up a long, gradual hill now, just as we were during my son's sixth grade year. It was getting harder to manage his educational needs by homeschooling. He was beginning to have difficulty letting me be teacher and mom, and we made the decision to enroll him in school for seventh grade. He also decided, leading into that year, that he wanted to go to West Point.

"We can see the top of the hill from here," encourages a man watching and cheering. So can I. I have to keep going steadily to get there. No time to rest, but no matter. I am feeling fine, and I know things will get a little easier very soon. Just like I felt at the end of sixth grade.

I cross the halfway point with no desire at all to turn in and go back to the start. Runners who have nearly finished, including my son, have already begun turning toward the end line. Even my friends who are running and walking have already passed that way; I cannot find their faces in the crowd coming toward me.

I can do this. I can walk that far.

It is encouraging to see those who are nearly finished. It reminds me of the encouragement we can experience by paying attention to the lives of those who have gone before. Some of them smile back at me as I walk joyfully on at the end of the line. I haven't stopped smiling yet or thanking those who cheer or serve water.

Seventh and eighth grade. Pretty level ground, not too challenging. Mile 4; 60 minutes. Now we're moving into high school, and headed up another long hill. Algebra II. That was tough. No time to slow down, though. No time to go back to reinforce earlier math concepts that may have been insufficiently mastered. Keep moving. Keep up the pace.

Somewhere between Mile 4 and Mile 5 there is a turn with a water station. The couple who were behind me have taken a shortcut and are now just ahead of me. Walking with their iPods, they haven't heard me behind them. We're all still keeping our fifteen-minute-mile pace. I hear the man say to the folks at the water table, "We're the last ones." Then he makes the turn and sees me. "I thought you were going to turn back?" (I had mentioned that early on, when we once made eye contact and he took out his earbuds.)

"No. I'm going to finish. Finishing is what counts." I smile and we exchange thumbs-up signs.

I am so grateful to be able to do this, to have opportunity, to have health, to have freedom. It means so much to be doing this along with my son, though he is far ahead of me. I continue my reflections. I'm almost to the five-mile point, which by my parallel counting system means the end of tenth grade. Now things will get really serious.

The couple ahead of me see their son now. Only a few runners or walkers are still on the course, but he has finished the last turn about a mile ahead of them and is headed for the last mile of the course.

I get two cups of water at this station, but barely sip. My stomach cramps a bit when I swallow a usual amount of water. I carry the cups and simply keep my mouth and lips moist. I feel fine. I've only taken one deep breath, and I haven't changed my pace at all, yet. Sure enough, at five miles I've been moving for seventy-five minutes.

Interestingly, during the eleventh grade year of my walk, I'm passing the place where my son worked as a lifeguard, before his eleventh grade year. And this is the year when the college decisions get serious. The letters to be written for West Point nominations have to go out. Twelfth grade, and interviews and college visits begin. Acceptance at The Citadel. Still waiting for word from West Point. Visit to West Point as a candidate.

Now I take my first step out of rhythm. A long hill is facing me, steeper than the others on the route. I feel a bit dizzy, and decide to slow my pace a bit. Finishing is what matters. So I pause for a beat, then start moving on up the hill at a slower rate.

I can do this. I can walk that far.

I hear my son's voice calling in greeting, and I look up to see him coming to meet me, along with his girlfriend. Some time around eleventh grade I realized that my little boy had become a young man. Now that young man is coming to meet me, to encourage me as I finish this race. I knew he would, and I knew he would ask to carry my things for me. I give him all but my flag.

We don't get to see our children become all they can be unless we finish the race. Taking shortcuts shortchanges us and those who follow us. I have paced myself; I have kept on walking; I have paid attention to my call and stayed on course. Because of this, my son has been able to go ahead of me, at his much faster pace, running instead of walking, following the call on his life. I could not run for him; I could not even run with him. But I could make it possible for him to run.

The last turn is in sight. My pace quickens again. Holding my flag, I make the turn and cross to the other side of the street. I have a specific task in mind.

Reading the signs on the roadside, I watch as the dates grow later. I'm looking for March 2010. I find the name I'm looking for. Robert Collins, from Tyrone, Georgia. KIA. He was 24. The sign doesn't say so, but he graduated from West Point in 2008. He was a close friend of dear friends of mine.

I kneel in front of the sign, with its image of the boots, rifle and helmet of a fallen Soldier. I say a brief prayer and plant my flag in the ground next to the sign post. I had determined to do this at the beginning of the race, but was on the wrong side of the crowd during the first few moments, when I was still trying to run the race at someone else's pace. So I carried Robert's flag for the duration. How could I not finish? I have done so little, so much less than the last full measure of devotion. Now I have completed my race, for today, and I have paid my respects.

I rise up and see the finish line ahead. The time is exactly right. I have paced myself. I have planned to finish, and to finish by 10:00. It is 10:00 as I cross the line, and the last "beep" of the day registers at the scoring table.

I won!

CHAPTER 2
People Say the Darnedest Things
(a collection of ridiculous comments)

Everyone has an opinion, and he or she isn't afraid to share it with you when the subject is your child's college choice. The West Point Moms have heard all kinds of comments, from simply stupid to beyond absurd. It's hard enough sending a kid to West Point to train to be a leader and war fighter for the United States Army without being bombarded by insensitivity from the uninformed or ignorant. Sometimes we West Point Moms forget that at one point, we didn't know very much about the Academy, either. Those of us who came from non-military backgrounds had a steep learning curve. We cannot really expect the general public to "get it" when it comes to West Point.

However, while the public might not "get it," surely they realize that some of their comments to us are insipid, rude, and generally in poor taste. Some people really should know better (e.g., high school guidance counselors). Moms deal with these comments in a variety of ways. The Southern moms might shake their heads and utter, "Bless her heart."

Some other moms have reported more confrontational exchanges. Some choose to take such comments as opportunities to educate the offenders, while others just walk away. Personally, I have a hard time keeping my mouth shut and have been known to "overly explain" a topic, whether the learner has listener's fatigue or not. After four years as a West Point Mom, though, I'm figuring out that not everyone appreciates the fountain of information that I am.

The moms have put together some of our more memorable exchanges with friends (or ex-friends, depending on how the mom responded to the comment). Here are a few of our favorites, grouped into categories because there are just so many ways that people misunderstand the West Point experience.

Though West Point was fortified as a military post by George Washington himself in 1778, and the United States Military Academy was established by Thomas Jefferson in 1802, many people do not know what it is or even where it is located. These people say things like:

- "West Point? Never heard of it."
- "Isn't that a military school?"
- "That's in Virginia, right?"
- "Is that in Texas?"
- "Where in California is West Point College?"
- "West Point is in New York? Then it should be called East Point."
- "Oh, I never knew there was a school there. How long has it been in operation?"

Apparently there is a common misconception that West

Point is some sort of reform school where wayward youth get sent to be straightened out, rather than a prestigious liberal arts institution that regularly produces scholars of the highest caliber in a wide range of fields of study. People with that idea ask:

- "Oh, is he going there because he wasn't able to get into a regular college?"

- From the school counselor: "He should go to community college first so he has a chance to experience real college."

- "I didn't realize he'd gotten in so much trouble to be sent there."

- "How is West Point one of the top colleges? How is that possible?"

- "My son couldn't get into a real college either. I'm so sorry for you. Maybe my kid could go there, too."

- (To a soon-to-be cadet) "Oh be quiet; you're not even going to college."

- "You are too smart to go there!"

A failure to understand the purpose of the Academy leads people to ask questions about our children going to war. These people simply don't understand that cadets are receiving the best training in the world specifically so that they can be best prepared to lead troops "to support and defend the Constitution of the United States against all enemies, foreign and domestic" (the Soldier's enlistment oath).

- "Don't die."

- "Why did you let him apply if you don't want him to deploy?"

- "He won't ever have to go to war, right, since he is an officer?"

- "Does he know he has to serve in the Army when he's done?"

- "Don't worry about her getting shot at; they always put their officers in a safe place to protect them."

- "You're going to let her kill people?"

- "He gets to choose if he wants to serve or not after graduation, right?"

The demands of military training are a mystery to civilians. The year-round training at West Point comes as a surprise to these folks. They ask:

- "What do you mean they don't get the summer off?"

- "They do military training and academics? How does that work?"

- "Oh, that's nice... do they have ROTC (Reserve Officer Training Corps) there?"

- "Why is it so long? OCS (Officer Candidate School) is only a few months."

Similar to the misunderstanding about the service expected of USMA graduates is the misunderstanding about how their education is funded. While cadets pay no tuition at the Academy, they do pay for their schooling. They give up significant freedoms to submit themselves to the authority, discipline, and training of the Army, not only for the four years at West Point, but for at least eight years afterward. Still, because it is such a unique opportunity, most people don't understand this, so they comment:

- "Did he apply there so you wouldn't have to pay for college?"

- "I guess that's why you don't have to work, since he's being paid to go to school."

- "What does it cost to go there?"

- "You are sure lucky you don't have to pay for his education."

- "Free ride—that must be nice; wish we could get a deal like that."

- "Is she getting any scholarship money to play for them?"

- "I just don't understand how that works; how can they afford to just give away an education like that? It's nice to see my tax money going to such crap."

There is confusion about which branches of service do which jobs, and that extends to their respective service academies as well. Here are some of the rumors believed by people who have shared their thoughts with other West Point moms.

- "West Point isn't that hard to get into. The Air Force is harder."

- "Is that for the Marines? (or Navy?) (or Air Force?)"

- "West Point has mostly humanities majors and Navy has mostly engineering majors."

- "My son is going to apply for the Naval Academy; it's much harder to get into. We are a Navy family."
  —"Oh, when did you serve?"—"Oh, I wasn't ever in the Navy."

Some people are confused about who makes the decision to attend a service academy. West Point moms have no misunderstandings in this area, having seen all the work their sons and daughters did to get appointed to the Academy. Other folks without that experience ask questions like:

- "And you're going to let him do this?"

- "Why would you want your son to go there? I can't imagine sending my son there. You know he will go to war don't you? I can't believe you would allow him to do that!"

- "_____ (insert name of your neighbor's perfect child) wanted to go there, but I wouldn't let him."

Finally, there are just random remarks that seem to arise out of the particular concerns of the people who make them. Some of these are made with good intentions, but some are just downright mean.

- "I think your kid will be a good fit there, with all the discipline he's used to, being in a military family."

- "Does he love it there?"

- "I truly understand how hard it was for you to leave your son. I did the same at the state university last year."

- From Grandma: "I'm afraid they're going to take him and make a man out of him."

- After Cow Commitment: "I'm so sorry; I really have no idea how you must feel."

- "I hear they have had to lower their standards to get students."

- "That's no place for a girl."
- "God will forgive him for his decision."
- "Do you mind your son hanging out with all those baby killers?"
- "In order to get into any of the academies, it's who you know, who you know, and who you know."
- "Don't worry; I'll get some guys in my office to talk him out of it."
- "My son is a saver, not a killer."
- "Have you come to regret your child's decision to attend West Point yet?"

When people ask if these things were really said, I just shake my head. You can't make this stuff up. Please use the space below, though, to write in your own experiences with stupid comments.

CHAPTER 3
Helicopters
(letting go)

When I took my firstborn (not my cadet) to the premier educational institution in our home state of Georgia, orientation was as much for the parents as for the students. I sat in the semi-darkness awaiting the presentation. Suddenly, I thought we were under attack! The sound of dozens of helicopters filled the air! The orientation session was titled "How to Avoid Being a Helicopter Parent." This was a new term for me.

I learned there are two types of helicopter parents: 1) Those who hover constantly, ready to help, fix, navigate, negotiate and basically save; and 2) Those who rapidly sweep in for the rescue. That's my job, right? I've done several versions of "mommy-fix-it" since becoming a mom. Apparently this college thought 18-year-olds were capable (ha!) of dealing with the situations life could throw at them.

They were right. If we back off, our kids will figure things out. They have to.

West Point is a "no-fly zone" for helicopter parents. It's not that our kids don't need or even want our advice—they might. It's that they are adults and members of the United States Army. They may not look or act like grownups to us, but they are. We do them a terrible disservice when we do not allow them to figure out problems for themselves.

Sure, there are times we do need to "mom." If my cadet were injured and in the hospital, you better believe I would either be calling the doctor or flying up there—or both. Plebe year, as a Southern born and raised boy, my son was freezing his keister off in October. He called and implored me to send long underwear ASAP. I could've sent him websites to order online, or directed him to the PX; however, I sent the underwear.

When he asked how to get an absentee ballot, I wanted to fill out the paperwork and have it sent to him. Instead, I sent a link to the county website and told him he could read about it and figure it out. I was so pleased when I learned he had actually done it and had voted! You have to decide how much you're willing to do.

For almost any West Point-related issue, however, there is already a protocol. It's called "the Chain of Command." Cadets learn about the importance of "the Chain" on R-Day. Those who don't follow it end up with issues. For example, a New Cadet with some blistered feet needs to tell the Chain. If the Chain doesn't know what's going on, they cannot help cadets with whatever the problem is.

With the technology resources we have, cadets are frequently asking moms what to do instead of asking the Chain. Perhaps they don't want to be viewed as ignorant. They are in this position, though, to learn to depend on the Chain of Command. One day, their subordinates will learn to trust them as well, as they become part of the Chain.

Here are some examples of things that can go wrong at West Point and what to do:

- Your cadet loses his wallet: Contact Chain.

- Your cadet loses uniform pieces: Contact Chain.

- Your cadet's flight is going to be late: Contact Chain.

- Your cadet misses the train: Contact Chain.

- Your cadet doesn't know where sick call is: Contact Chain.

- Your cadet needs Oreo Balls: Contact Mom.

CHAPTER 4

Now What?

(from appointment to the Point)

After months (often years) of hard work, your son or daughter has received an appointment to the United States Military Academy. Congratulations, Mom! R-Day (the day your Cadet Candidate reports to West Point) is months away; what do you do now? Because the purpose of this book is to support you as a mom so that you are better prepared to support your cadet, we want to help you enjoy the last few months of "normal" with as little stress as possible. You definitely have some work to do in order to be prepared for R-Day, but it's all doable, and it doesn't need to be daunting.

Lists are useful when they're realistic. Communication from West Point does not always give the initial impression of being very realistic, but we've broken down the Cadet Candidate instructions into a list so you can see that it's all manageable.

Paperwork

Your Cadet Candidate received a mailing from West Point with an official title something like "Directions for Cadets

Offered Admission." We know that some moms have Cadet Candidates who have lived life in the adult world—even the military world—and those Candidates can read and translate Army-speak into instructions that can be followed by mere mortals. However, if your Cadet Candidate is still finishing up high school or time in a civilian college, you're probably going to have to wade together through all the forms. At the very least, you will need to locate paperwork (e.g., birth certificate or immunization records).

Medical

In addition to locating medical paperwork, you may be called upon to help schedule medical visits. Your Cadet Candidate has already had the physical and eye examinations required for application, but now there are immunizations and blood tests required as well. Some of these are the same as those that would be necessary for a civilian student planning to live in a college dormitory, but the Army requires more extensive shots and other certifications. For example, if your child had a particular childhood disease and therefore has not received an immunization for that disease, a blood test must confirm the presence of immune factors confirming that fact. Some of this work can be completed in a doctor's office, but you may have to go to a public health clinic, travel clinic, or hospital to get all the requirements completed.

If you haven't done so before, you might use this process as a teaching opportunity. Communicating with medical personnel is not something most eighteen-year-olds have a lot of experience doing. It's one of those life skills that doesn't fit neatly into school curriculum, and we tend to do it for our children when they're living at home. Once they leave home they need to know how to do it, though, and an appointment to West Point gives you a ready-made opportunity to instruct your child in one more area before you hand off the lead to the Army.

Do not be surprised or concerned if, after completing and submitting the immunization paperwork, an additional envelope arrives from DoDMERB (the Department of Defense Medical Examination Review Board) stating that there is a discrepancy of some sort in the forms submitted. It usually means a box didn't get checked that needs to be checked, and a quick trip to the doctor's office or call to the clinic can resolve the matter. If your Cadet Candidate receives such a discrepancy letter, don't hesitate to call DoDMERB at the contact number provided if you are unsure of how to respond; the letters are written with a lot of standard language and can be difficult to understand, but the people at DoDMERB are generally helpful in clarifying these matters. If your child is over the age of eighteen, expect that this information will have to be discussed with him or her rather than you; that's a Federal law.

Physical

There are instructions and even illustrations in the material your Cadet Candidate received, detailing exercises and training regimens to prepare for West Point. Specifically, this is to get ready for the first summer's Cadet Basic Training (CBT, also known as "Beast Barracks"). The jury remains out on how best to respond to this information, but we think it is best for you to let your child make that decision. You may hear about students following the instructions to the letter, gradually increasing running distance and time, push-up and sit-up counts. Running or walking (marching) with a pack and adding weight to the pack incrementally is also advised, as is training in heat in a managed way and paying attention to body hydration. Certainly all of these activities will help a Cadet Candidate to face the challenges of summer training at West Point.

Your Cadet Candidate may not be motivated to do all that training while still finishing life in the civilian world. It may be more important to say good-bye to friends and family and home by spending extra intentional time in all those special relationships and places. While you may not hear this course of action touted as the route to success, many cadets at West Point will tell you that once Cadet Candidates arrive at Beast and become New Cadets, the intense training will be difficult no matter how fit they are. This is because part of the purpose of Beast is to find New Cadets' limits and push them just a little further so that they learn to rely on the strength of the team and not on themselves alone. Bearing that in mind, Cadet Candidates may legitimately choose to finish civilian life well, on their own terms, while they are allowed to control how they spend their time, and the mental and emotional preparation they receive from this will help them to overcome the physical challenges of Beast.

Regardless of how they prepare, on R-Day New Cadets will be marching and carrying heavy packs for much of the day, and Beast training will be rigorous. Your Cadet Candidate is aware of this and will decide the best way to be ready.

Boots and Shoes

On your Cadet Candidate's admissions portal is a link for the "boot letter." This letter explains what kind of boots to purchase prior to reporting on R-Day. In addition to the boots, low quarters (black leather shoes of a specific brand) need to be purchased. On the surface, you'd think purchasing a pair of boots and a pair of shoes would be a pretty straightforward endeavor. Not so. Every year parents report chasing all over their state (and beyond) to find the boots and shoes for West Point. It can be very frustrating. But you are armed with information, so it doesn't have to be!

If you are not part of a military family, keep the boot letter with you when you shop. It authorizes you to be on post and to purchase in a Post Exchange (PX) or Uniform Store, all of which generally require military ID.

Post Exchanges, department stores operated for military personnel, are managed by the Army and Air Force Exchange Service (AAFES). As in any chain of department stores, each location's inventory is adjusted to local need. This means that not every PX will have the boots and shoes required by West Point. This also means that your very best option for locating the right shoes and boots and getting a good fit is at the West Point PX. If your son or daughter is visiting the Academy after accepting an appointment, purchase the footwear while there. However, if that's not an option, you can find the shoes and boots elsewhere.

If you live near a PX, you might find what you are looking for there. Often, however, the local PX has limited sizes and brands available. If you can't find what you need at the post nearest you, it's not necessary to drive all over your region. Have your Cadet Candidate try on what is available to get an idea of proper sizing. A helpful clerk might be willing to check with other post or base exchanges which can mail the boots or shoes to you at home. Also, once size is determined, you can order online at the All Services Exchange online store (www.shopmyexchange.com). If trying on shoes at a local PX isn't an option, the nice people at AAFES will help you determine over the phone what sizes to buy.

If your Cadet Candidate is like most other young people, the footwear of choice is tennis shoes or flip-flops. The reason West Point authorizes the early purchase of the shoes and boots is so the Cadet Candidate can break them in. It's not really the shoes that need breaking in: it's the feet. Kids are not used to wearing boots or dress shoes for long periods of time. It's worth noting this and explaining it to your Cadet Candidate. Keep the chopper in the hangar, though; you don't need to hover overhead to see if the shoes or the feet get broken in. As with the physical training, it's up to your Cadet Candidate to follow the instructions or not, and it's your cadet's feet that will bear the consequences of that decision.

Travel

Your Cadet Candidate may fly at USMA's expense into New York City the day before R-Day, stay overnight, and be transported first thing Monday morning to West Point (yes, without you, but also without you paying for the trip). If your Cadet Candidate travels with the family, the Candidate's travel expenses will be reimbursed by the Academy. Information about all of this is in the "Directions" package mailed to your Cadet Candidate. Your cadet will fill out forms during Beast to request reimbursement, and the money will then be deposited into a cadet account. (These accounts are described more fully in our "Funny Money" chapter.) You will likely never see it.

If you are going to travel to R-Day, figure out your travel plans. Will you drive? While West Point is somewhat hidden away along the Hudson, it is only an hour from New York City and only a short distance from several interstate highways. That is to say, you can get there by car and airport service is very convenient as well. If you choose to fly, your limitations are based on the options you have from your originating airport. Those living near major hubs have more choices. There are five airports that serve the West Point area. Newark (airport code EWR) is in Newark, NJ; in New York City are LaGuardia (LGA) and JFK (JFK). Closer to West Point, and much less congested, is Westchester County Airport (HPN), usually called by the name of the town where it is located, White Plains. The very closest and easiest to navigate is Stewart (SWF), in Newburgh. Because I live in Atlanta (a major airline hub), I can fly into any of those airports. I choose Stewart when the price is right because it is the closest airport to West Point. However, I have friends who choose JFK because they think it's exciting to drive through New York City! Your choice can be based on your preferences. You can get lots of opinions and advice, if you want, by asking the West Point Moms on Facebook. More information about that is at the end of this chapter.

Once you get to New York, where are you going to stay? Some parents want to be as close to West Point as possible, so they book at the Thayer Hotel right on post. For some families, this is cost prohibitive. You have many lodging choices in the surrounding area and can make your decision based on what is important to your family (i.e., location, price, luxury, etc.). Highland Falls is the village closest to West Point—its Main Street leads directly into one of West Point's gates—and it offers a few hotel options. The next closest town is Fort Montgomery. Other towns you will hear parents talk about staying in include (but are not limited to) Central Valley, Newburgh, Fishkill, Nyack, Cornwall, Cold

Springs, Nanuet, and Mahwah. You might want to go ahead and book rooms for R-Day and A-Day if you're attending both and if you're sure of plans this far in advance.

Get Connected

You will hear us mention connecting online over and over in this book. We believe in social networking and in the power of "virtual support." If you want to be as informed as you can be, connecting to online resources is the way to do it. We suggest the following:

- If you don't already have one, set up a Facebook account now (www.facebook.com).

- "Like" the official USMA Parents' Facebook page (www.facebook.com/WestPointParents). This is where you will find both pictures and links to more pictures of your cadet during Beast and the Academic Year.

- Join West Point Moms on Facebook (www.facebook. com/WestPointMoms). (It is a closed group and you won't be able to access the page until you're approved by the moderators.) This is an unofficial page just for moms of West Point cadets. Here you will find a sisterhood of women who have been there, done that, and are ready to help you navigate the route to and through your 47-month adventure. Pretty much any question you have is fair game for the moms. If no one has an answer to your question, these ladies know how to find it for you.

- "Like" the West Point Commandant's Facebook page (www.facebook.com/pages/BG-Theodore-Martin/126845184070576). The Commandant loves to take cadet pictures and post them. NOTE: Commandants do leave West Point, and new Coms replace them. Since this Facebook page is specifically linked to General Martin's name, in a few years you may instead need to "like" a page in the name of a new Commandant. You will be able to find his name on the West Point website.

• Get to know the West Point website (www.USMA. edu). There is a wealth of great information on this page. You can find the answer to pretty much anything officially related to West Point on this site. If you can't find it here, you can ask on either West Point Parents or West Point Moms on Facebook. Someone will have an answer for you soon.

Now you've done everything you need to do to prepare to be the mom of a West Point cadet. Anything else? Oh, yes—sit back, relax, and enjoy the rest of the time your son or daughter is at home. You can do this: you're a West Point Mom!

CHAPTER 5
A Reception in Your Honor (*R-Day*)

Here's a place to tip our hats to the West Point Parents' Clubs. We hope they're all as good as ours, especially when it comes to supporting parents through R-Day and A-Day. We had committed leaders in our club who explained and described and illustrated and answered questions we didn't even know to ask. They remembered their own passage through the Stony Lonesome Gate (or whichever gate, but doesn't that name sound most appropriate?) to deposit their precious offspring in the jaws of the Beast, and they were eager to help us survive our own crucible with minimal collateral damage. One experienced mom even sent out a list of suggestions for the day, and every one of them was a good one. If you haven't tried out the parents' club in your area, check into it—even if the meetings are a bit of a drive from home, give them a try. You may find a lot of support at critical moments, and you'll definitely find other parents who understand what you're going through—which you absolutely will not find in most other places. For more information on parents' clubs, see our chapter titled "Get Involved."

For any readers who haven't learned yet, or who maybe never quite got the message, R = Reception, and A = Acceptance. Reception Day, generally the last Monday in June or first Monday in July, is the day your Cadet Candidate is received into the training program at West Point, and by the end of that day he or she is a New Cadet. It is the start of CBT (Cadet Basic Training), fondly known as "Beast Barracks" or simply "Beast." Beast officially ends with the March Back in early- to mid-August. Following that, the New Cadets are accepted into the Corps of Cadets at a review (parade) on Acceptance Day. On that day they finally drop the "New" designation and officially become Plebes.

"Reception" and "Acceptance" sound friendly enough, don't they? Receptions are nice events, with promises of good company, stimulating conversation, even tasty food. Hang on to that image, if it makes you feel better. Your son or daughter will be meeting some very good people on R-Day; conversation is pretty one-sided, but a lot will be learned; and at the end of the day there will be a meal in Washington Hall, where there is a beautiful dining room staffed by excellent cooks and wait staff. Of course, your New Cadet may not notice the luxuries of the day; they may be overshadowed by the need to move continually from one place to another while taking in a significant amount of new information. Surviving R-Day, for the New Cadets, means leaving the emotions out of it; there will be occasion for those later. Perhaps that will be the time to appreciate the more genteel aspects of the reception. Or not.

You, however, will not spend the day having yourself

rearranged to look as if you have no hair, no figure (or physique), no style, and no individuality. You will have plenty of time for gentility and possibly too much time for emotion. The better prepared you are for this day, the better off you'll be when it happens, and the more satisfied you'll be in looking back at it. Think of this section like you would a prepared childbirth class: we're going to tell you some things that might make no sense now, but when you get into labor you'll understand and you'll be oh, so glad you know.

To moms who do not accompany their Cadet Candidates to R-Day: You have done well. You have brought up a young person who is capable of traveling alone to a probably unfamiliar place, managing logistics on a cross-country (or international) trip, arriving on time to a critically important meeting, and accepting personally the mental and emotional challenges of it all. Know this, too: everything that happens at West Point on that day can be successfully completed by an unaccompanied seventeen-year-old. The packet of information sent to those who accept their appointment includes all the maps, directions, instructions, and schedules they will need. The whole campus is set up to direct people to the right place on R-Day, and once a candidate finds the first line to stand in, things pretty much proceed as if on a conveyor belt. It's all a part of the system, and the system works. Don't worry. Worry only hurts you, and it doesn't help your cadet. Take care of yourself; you're an important part of the support team, even from far away. If you prefer to go through trials alone, plan to take some time on this day for yourself, to meditate, pray, paint, listen to music, or maybe write a letter to your New Cadet—whatever feeds your spirit. If you are a social person, try to get together with another Academy parent on that day, if you can. Again, the Parents' Clubs are great for this, as a place to connect with those who've been there and done that, and you might also find support online from an experienced friend or an online forum. Even a parent who went through R-Day years ago will remember well either being there or NOT being there and will be able to support you if you want company as you get through that first day. It's probably a good idea, whether you're a loner or a party girl, to have someone to talk to during the day; the support of community is invaluable when going through such a challenging time. You will read about a good bit of information in this chapter; however, do not feel like you will be missing out because you did not see these events with your own eyes. All the information from the briefing with the leadership team will later be posted on the West Point website at www.USMA.edu.

To moms who go with their cadets to R-Day: This is one seriously big day. A little prep work will make it easier for you to navigate the physical, mental, and emotional challenges of the day. It's a long one, first of all; you'll be there for at least twelve hours unless your cadet is assigned one of the latest report times (based on the last two digits of his or her Social Security number)—then maybe it'll only be ten hours. Plan to pack a small bag with a shoulder strap, to take the following:

- government-issued photo ID for all members of your party 16 years of age or older; you can't get on post without this

- car insurance and registration papers if you're driving in; the guards might inspect your car at the post gate

- map of West Point (this is in material your Cadet Candidate has received)

- schedule for R-Day (ditto)
- camera, if you like that sort of thing
- sunscreen
- lip balm
- bottled water
- tissues
- writing paper, envelopes, and stamps
- pens or pencils
- crayons or markers if you have young children along
- a puzzle book or deck of cards or other packable diversions
- healthy, age-appropriate, packable snacks that don't need refrigerating
- binoculars if you have them (don't buy any—someone will share if you ask)
- cash or credit card for purchasing lunch and/or dinner and all those souvenirs
- cell phones (for your party; cadets can't keep theirs during Beast)
- rain jacket(s) if rain is forecast

If this is your first time dealing with the military, you're about to be introduced to "hurry up and wait," the unofficial motto of the Army. As a rule of thumb, you want to think: Ten minutes early is on time; on time is late. There is a simple reason for this: Lots of people are moving at the same time to the same place. They all need to be in that place at once, but obviously they can't all arrive there simultaneously.

It takes time for a few hundred people to go through a doorway, for example, so being in line to go through, even ten minutes early, assures you that when you need to be on the other side of the doorway, you'll be there. On R-Day, plan to be in line at the gate at least half an hour earlier than you think you should be there. It usually doesn't take that long to clear security, but with over 1,000 Cadet Candidates and their entourages moving in two lanes, things can get bottle-necked, even with a staggered reporting time schedule. You'll be parking in a designated area and most likely walking a short distance to meet a shuttle bus. There's enough tension on this day without having to worry about being late.

After being shuttled to another line, usually at Eisenhower Hall, you'll stand, possibly for more than an hour, waiting your turn to get to the 90-second good-bye. The wait in line offers you the opportunity to chat with other parents and Cadet Candidates from around the country, gaze at the spectacular view of the campus, and enjoy some West Point-provided entertainment such as clowns and jugglers. This is also where the need for some of those items in your bag becomes apparent. You may or may not be in the sun and/or rain; you may or may not need to wipe an eye or a nose; you may or may not have been too nervous to eat breakfast, only to find that your stomach wakes up half an hour into the wait; you may or may not have children who are simply dying of thirst and/or boredom five minutes into the wait.

Now, about that 90-second good-bye: First of all, 90 seconds at West Point means just that: Ninety. Seconds. It's not a minute, as in, "I'll be there in a minute," which can mean half an hour. You will walk with your young person into an auditorium, after having waited in that serpentine line seemingly for hours; there will be a short (much too short) briefing to let you know what comes next; an officer will say something like, "Cadet Candidates, you have 90 seconds to say your good-byes and proceed to the exit to my left," and you will have 90 seconds for a hug, a kiss, and a final word. You will share this 90 seconds with all in your party; the 90 seconds applies to the cadet, not to each person who is there for the farewell. I have a large family, so there were seven hugs to get into that literal minute and a half. Our advice: The adieus and final words should already have happened by this time. Spend your time leading up to R-Day in meaningful ways, taking opportunities to speak or write your farewells and good wishes while you may do so at your leisure. Also, realize that this is not good-bye forever, but only a temporary parting. With all that in mind, be brave, smile at your young adventurer so as to make a pleasant memory of your face, give a good strong—but quick—hug, and say your parting words, and listen to your cadet's. Then release your hold and let your child walk down the aisle and proceed to exit your view through the door to the officer's left.

After your Cadet Candidate disappears (it's really not forever, and realistically it's not for all that long a time), you and the other bereft families and friends in the auditorium will be directed to the kind of gathering we usually think of in association with the word "reception." It's a place where you can get a little something to eat and drink (usually donuts and fruit, coffee and juice), relax in air-conditioned comfort for a while, and even sit in a fairly comfortable chair, possibly in a room with a view. This is not all bad, see? Oh, and near the entrance, on your way from the auditorium to the reception, there's sure to be a big bowl full of... packets of tissues. Such nice people, these military folks; thoughtful, too. Restrooms (with mirrors for checking the status of your mascara) are nearby, as well.

In an area near the reception, there will be a few tables you should stop by, one of them being a place to get the actual mailing address for your New Cadet during Beast. Company assignments aren't made until very close to R-Day, so specific information you need to send mail is not available until the actual day. Find the table. Get the piece of paper with the address. Put it in your wallet or in your own very safe place. You'll get a post office box number and a company assignment; company information is needed for mail delivery in the field during the second half of Beast. You'll want to know the company assignment later today at the Oath Ceremony, too. There may be other tables there, as well, with helpful information and always with helpful people. Most of these are volunteers, many of whom are West Point parents themselves, and they do want to help you get through the day.

After your party is sufficiently refreshed and regrouped (in a slightly but significantly smaller group), it's time to find things to take home and to do. Shoppers, start your engines. Collectors, open your bags. (Budgeters, guard your wallets.) This is the biggest shopping day of the year at West Point, and probably in Highland Falls, New York, as well. Of the two of us writing here, one is not a shopper, so we know the day can be survived without retail therapy. However, if you have a budget for this sort of thing, there are things to buy that are nice to have.

Like many of the wild rides at theme parks, this ride also empties into a gift shop. The entire ballroom of Eisenhower Hall is filled with tables offering just about any USMAthemed item you could imagine, allowing you to announce to the world that you have a cadet at West Point. The USMA Bookstore and the Cadet Store will have merchandise there, as will the gift shop from the off-campus West Point Museum. You'll have the option of buying regular items that declare West Point affiliation, or those very special ones that declare you are a West Point Mom (or Dad or Sibling or Grandparent). Some of these items, especially those with class year on them, are only available on R-Day, so if you see something you really have to have, you might want to go ahead and get it. You don't really know if it will still be available on your next visit to West Point.

If you are interested in football tickets you'll be able to get the information for purchasing those in this room as well. Representatives will be on hand to explain the different package options so you will be ready when the season begins. Go Army, Beat Navy!

Not all the tables in Eisenhower Hall are there to help you spend money. Many parents' clubs from around the country set up to be there just to help you in general. If your club is there, find them; these are folks who are eager to answer questions and provide support today and throughout your West Point experience. They have more tissues, and some offer bottled water and cookies. If you don't find your group there, that's okay, too; whichever parents' clubs are there will be happy to adopt you for the day.

After you've completed your tour of the ballroom, a lot depends on your group. You may want to stay together; you may have some who want to go off alone and re-join later. The Academy is a safe place to be; that's not an illusion. If someone needs some solitude, follow your family's usual plans about checking in while out and about, but there are places on campus both off and on the beaten path to grab a little quiet during the day. Check out the many seating areas facing the Hudson, or perhaps stroll down toward Flirtation Walk (check your map). The grounds are beautiful; enjoy them!

Some families take this time to sit at a bench or table somewhere and write the first letter to their New Cadet. (For suggestions on writing, see our chapter, "You've Got Mail!") This day is intense for everyone, but it's really all about the New Cadets. Writing a note now can give you an opportunity to re-set the emotions from "Ouch, this really hurts," to "I am proud of you." Letters may be mailed conveniently from the drop box in Eisenhower Hall or the West Point Post Office near Thayer Gate (see map).

If there are others in your party, this is also a chance to talk about making that emotional transition. Everyone will process all this differently, even within your own family. Don't be surprised by a sibling who thinks it's no big deal or by one who cries off and on throughout the day. Each of you has a special way of relating to the one you just hugged good-bye, so each of you will have a unique way of dealing with the separation. Moms don't usually need to be reminded to support the family emotionally, but do remember to do that today, and to allow them to support you as well.

Some families need a break from all the excitement and choose to go off-post for a bit. Just outside Thayer Gate is the quaint little village of Highland Falls, which does offer a few pleasantries for families. On your right after you exit Thayer Gate, USAA has a bank branch office. This is important to you because you can get a free West Point Parent tote bag there during R-Day weekend. The West Point Museum and Gift Shop are also close by, on the left out of the gate. This museum boasts the largest collection of militaria in the Western Hemisphere. The West Point Visitors Center, which is attached to the museum, has model cadet rooms on display. There's a good-sized gift shop there, too, to buy goodies if you like. Next door to the Visitors Center, there is a McDonald's in case the little ones in your party can't get through the day without Chicken McNuggets. Up on Main Street you'll find a Dunkin' Donuts and a few other small restaurants, and also a really yummy Ice Cream Shoppe. The shopping on Main Street, for this day, is at Vasily's; it's basically a West Point souvenir shop that can customize your purchases with embroidery. If you wrote to your New Cadet and didn't mail on post, the Highland Falls Post Office is at the other end of Main Street; leaving Thayer Gate, stay to the right and the Highland Falls Post Office is on the right just before Mountain Avenue. Remember! If you go off post on R-Day, be sure to allow plenty of time to get back through security, find parking, and walk or locate a shuttle before the next event you want to catch on post. Remember that there are hundreds of other people with similar ideas, and lines may be long at the gate, the shuttle, and the door of the building you want to enter.

You can eat and shop conveniently on post, as well, even right "on campus." Grant Hall houses a short-order cafeteria; sandwiches and pizza and drinks are available there, and it's right in the Academy complex. There is a Post Exchange near Stony Lonesome Gate with a Taco Bell and a Burger King, and a Subway is located beyond the cemetery near the Post Chapel (consult your map). The West Point Club is open for lunch, and if you're really feeling like a special meal the Thayer Hotel may be able to seat you. For shopping, the permanent locations of the Cadet Store ("C-Store") and the USMA Bookstore are, of course, on post; the C-Store is in Building 606 and the Bookstore is in Thayer Hall.

If your group is more interested in the human scenery of the day than the historic and commercial wonders of the area, there are gathering places where you can catch glimpses of New Cadets in various stages of transformation. Stake out a piece of sidewalk for your group outside Grant or Thayer Hall for the best view, but any place not cordoned off is fair game. Some families spend much of the day sitting and watching New Cadets move through from building to building, noting progress as New Cadets receive uniforms and duffel bags and haircuts and other delights. You might even see your own very special New Cadet, but be prepared—they all look an awful lot alike once they're dressed the same, cleared of hair, and laden with bags of gear. This is the beginning of your 47-month "Where's Waldo?" game. One caution here: this day can be rough emotionally on moms and on New Cadets. Consider enjoying all that the day has to offer, rather than stalking your cadet. Some New Cadets have a tougher time if they do see their parents, and you don't want to be the cause of any additional stress on this oh-so-stressful day.

There is a briefing for parents toward the end of the afternoon (check the schedule that arrived in the mail or the one you picked up at Eisenhower Hall earlier in the day), where the Superintendent, Commandant, and Dean will speak to you about what you already know (that your cadet is wonderful) and what you want to know (what your cadet will be doing this summer and beyond). The notes from this briefing will be posted online at www.USMA.edu within a few days after R-Day, so you may refer to them there rather than stressing about taking notes during the talks. After this meeting it will be time to find a place to watch the Oath Ceremony.

Some time during the day your son or daughter will have read and signed an oath to serve the United States of America at the United States Military Academy. The Oath Ceremony is a formal recognition of that commitment, where the incoming class stands together for the first time as a body and repeats the oath in unison. Oh, my goodness, how much they've learned in this one day. They'll appear dressed in "white over gray"—white short-sleeved shirt, gray slacks—with white gloves and those shiny black shoes you had to buy at an Army post last spring. They can march in formation, they can stand at attention, they can stay silent in company, and they can salute. It's possible that yours will be one who can also make eye contact to let you know things are fine. They march by company, and you'll know your cadet's company by the mailing address you got in the morning (you picked it up in Eisenhower Hall, after the 90-second good-bye). Company guidons (small flags, arranged alphabetically along The Plain, where the parade is held) mark the place where each company will stop and stand. If you can find your New Cadet's company guidon and sit or stand near it, you may indeed get a final glimpse of your Waldo at the close of the day. Afterwards, the newly sworn-in New Cadets march away to have their first dinner in Washington Hall. Most parents will stay and watch the last white over gray disappear through the arched doorway, and the sound of those huge wooden doors closing behind the last cadet is a sound to echo in memories for a long time.

Well. That was a day, then. Time to get people and things together and start marching. You've officially begun your Beast summer!

CHAPTER 6

Slaying the Beast— as a Mom
(surviving Beast summer)

The Corps has a term, not in our Lingo list, for getting through Beast Barracks successfully. They call it "Slaying the Beast." When the doors close on Washington Hall after the Oath Ceremony, your Beast summer truly begins, and you get to try your hand at a bit of slaying. You've survived the initial skirmish. Now you're ready for the fight.

For some of us, this is when the emotions let loose. If that's your experience, go ahead and cry; if you haven't already done so, it's high time! There will probably be another mom nearby who won't mind your tears; maybe you can even help each other talk through the moment. It's part of the West Point Moms' bonding, and you may as well start that, too, if you haven't already.

You can't sit there forever, though, staring at the Million Dollar View through blurred bifocals. So when you're ready, use some of those tissues you picked up in the Eisenhower lobby or ballroom, blow your nose, wipe your eyes, and start marching. Chin up, girls! We can do this. We can walk that far.

Food. You might as well have a bite; the others in your party will be hungry by this time of the day. Eat something good for you, not only comfort food. You want to stay fit; you're in training now. Drink your water. (How much water have you lost today in sweat and tears, hmm?)

If you haven't done it yet, the supper table is a good place to write a first note to your New Cadet. Everyone can write and put notes in lots of envelopes if you like. That makes for more "presents" to be opened at mail call, or whenever your New Cadet will have time to open presents. If you're driving home and have already left West Point, you might mail an envelope from a post office along the way.

During the next few weeks you'll face lots of challenges. Here are a few ideas for getting through them.

The days are long during Beast summer, but they are limited in number. Make a chart with the number of days left until A-Day or whatever day you'll next see your cadet. Each day you can mark off a day on the chart and have a visual reminder that you're that much closer. You can mark each day with a smiley or frownie face to chart how you're doing, if you're scientifically inclined. For children, a fun way to mark the time is to make a paper chain, one link for each day, representing how long it will be before seeing big brother or sister again. Each morning, or each night at bedtime, a link can be removed and tossed away, shortening the chain and hopefully lightening the heart a little as well.

Stay in touch with friends, girlfriend or boyfriend, and family who are also in touch with your New Cadet. Share letters with each other so everyone gets to hear the news, even if it's the same news over and over. One note here, though: if you start to feel weary of sharing that news over and over, don't feel a bit bad about not answering the phone or otherwise taking time for yourself, for your private thoughts and feelings. There is a void in your life because someone very important is missing from your daily activities. You will very likely need some time alone to adjust and to process emotions. Take what you need to take care of yourself. (Moms are not always good at that, are we?)

You may find it helpful, as you take care of yourself, to see pictures of what's going on at West Point during Beast Barracks. Once upon a time, before about 2009, pictures of cadets were only shared by parents who happened to be at West Point during the summer for some official reason. That's one reason the West Point Moms group started on Facebook, actually. Now, in much more enlightened times, pictures are posted regularly from official West Point sources on a very frequent basis, so you can play Where's Waldo? on Facebook and your chances of finding your own Waldo are pretty good. In addition to the West Point Moms page on www.facebook.com, there are pages there for West Point Dads and West Point Parents; additionally, the Dean and Superintendent have pages you can join (Dean of Academics at West Point; Superintendent of West Point), and there is a page called West Point – The U.S. Military Academy. Try not to get too addicted to looking. (Remember to drink your water, at least.) Seriously, it is easy to forget other responsibilities while looking for that familiar face you miss so much; make conscious efforts to stay familiar to the faces still at home with you, too.

From a mom's perspective, there are three critical events on the schedule during Beast summer, and the approximate dates of those will be given to you in the Superintendent's briefing on R-Day (and posted online afterward). The three events are the First Phone Call, the Ice Cream Social, and the third phone call. These are the three planned times that your New Cadet will have permission to make a phone call.

Note that the First Phone Call is capitalized; these distinctions come from the heart, not from official spellings, and the First Phone Call looms huge in a mom's heart. It is the first time after R-Day that you'll hear your cadet's voice and be able to do all that super-detective work you do as a mom. (Does he sound discouraged, or just tired? Is she really, really okay? Was that a hesitation, or just a breath, when he responded to that question?) On the up-side, it may be a chance to hear a familiar laugh or a favorite phrase that you've missed hearing for many days, a little music for your heart to treasure and replay later. Your cadet will have the opportunity to call you during a particular week, early in Beast; the exact time and date will not be announced in advance because its timing depends on cadet duties, squad performance, company activities, phone availability, and any number of other factors. Trust the system and wait as patiently as you can. Cadre will manage all the details and ensure that your cadet will get a phone call in; remember that the system works for the good of the whole, though, not for the good of any individual cadet—or mom.

You'll have to bear that in mind during the call, too, because the time will be strictly limited. New Cadets generally get one phone call that may last ten (West Point) minutes—600 seconds. They can't break up the time to call more than one person, and they absolutely cannot go over time. Other cadets will be waiting to use the same phone, and the mission must be completed in a specified period of time. Relish your ten minutes; they are precious; but don't let your feelings be hurt by an abrupt end to the visit. One way to avoid an awkward ending is to treat the call like you would treat a cell phone call while driving toward a place where you always lose signal: say the most important things early, including "I love you," and a just-in-case farewell, and then when your New Cadet says the time is up, you can just toss in a "Love you—'Bye!" Also realize that a member of cadre may be within hearing distance, so your cadet's conversation may seem a bit terse or limited. These are skills you'll need often, not only during the super-busy West Point years, but also during the time afterward when your Soldier calls home.

About halfway through Beast, New Cadets will have an opportunity to attend an ice cream social in the home of a coach or an instructor or a sponsor family. The number of cadets at a particular residence will vary, based on the hosts' limitations. The gathering is usually on a Sunday afternoon, as cadet duties are reduced on Sundays, even during Beast. Hosts may offer a meal, television, video games, or movies in addition to ice cream. More important than the ice cream, though, is the fact that at the Ice Cream Social, phones and computers will be available for cadets' use, with the only usage restriction being the need to share with other cadets. So the Ice Cream Social is a big deal for you as well, because you'll be able to visit long-distance with your New Cadet fairly freely.

Here's a fun idea for that visit: have your own Ice Cream Social! You'll have the definite date, though not a precise time, from the Superintendent's briefing. Invite friends and/or family of your New Cadet to bring ice cream and hang around waiting to hear from the remote guest of honor. If it suits, put the cadet on speaker phone when the call arrives, so family and guests will get a chance not only to hear that dear voice, but to reply as well. This can be a bit difficult to manage if you have a large group, since it requires you all to stay silent except for the one person speaking at a given time. However, if your cadet's call time is not strictly limited, you might be able to pass the phone around for everyone chat individually. At our Ice Cream Social, I posted printouts from the Superintendent's briefing, for guests to get an idea of what exactly their friend had signed up to do. We took pictures of friends & family in various silly poses, some in military gear. I even dressed like an R-Day cadet and posed for a push-up photo to send to the New Cadet later. Yes, I really donned long black shorts, white undershirt, black socks & black dress shoes. Note that I posed, though—I can't do a real push-up.

Even if you can't do a real push-up, over the course of the summer, as much as possible, try to exercise and get your rest. If you take care of yourself you'll feel better physically, but also emotionally, and you need the emotional support of a healthy body. Some moms use this summer's separation as a motivation to get in better shape, walking or running to burn off anxiety, rest the eyes from the computer monitor, and feel a sense of connection with that New Cadet who is walking or running for a good portion of every day. If you do increase your exercise this summer, you'll look all the more smashing in that gown you'll be wearing to the formal banquet at Plebe Parent Weekend next spring!

Oh, and the third phone call—it will be much like the first, scheduled at Cadre's discretion during a particular week, and limited to a ten-minute visit. If things are going well for your cadet, this will be a time to confirm what you've been hoping—that things are beginning to make sense, duties are starting to feel routine, and some interesting and even humorous memories have been made. This will be your last checkpoint before March Back, when New Cadets return to campus and join their Academic Year companies. If things are not going well, try to remember (and remind your cadet) that you're both on the downhill slope by this point, almost finished with Cadet Basic Training. The anticipation of the close of Beast Barracks will likely give you and your New Cadet a lift during this visit.

Following this phone call, CBT moves to Camp Buckner for field training. The actual move out to Camp Buckner is usually done by helicopter, which is pretty cool and exciting for many cadets. Once in the field, this is when the mail may slow down. If you're writing letters (we hope you are), keep it up, but know that mail delivery is not neat and orderly when cadets are spread out in camps all over several hundred acres of terrain. Your cadet may receive letters in clumps or not at all, and conditions may not allow return letters to be written and sent. Of course, you also may get a letter written on the cardboard wrapper of an MRE or a bullet-riddled target from the rifle range. Ah, the little treasures our children send us!

The official close of CBT is a 12.5-mile march from Camp Buckner to the West Point campus—creatively called the March Back. New Cadets and Cadre carry all their gear from the field during this march. The weight, the distance, and the heat all contribute to make the march challenging. In the spirit of the Long Gray Line, though, graduates often join the marchers to encourage them on the way. The grads from the class 50 years previous make a special effort to be there during this event. Also, local citizens as well as West Point families show up with signs and flags to cheer for the "troops" along the route. Yes, you are authorized to go see this event, but you will be an observer, unless you're a grad yourself.

Reorgy begins immediately following March Back. Short for "reorganization," this is the time when cadets join their Academic Year (AY) companies, move into AY barracks with AY roommates, acquire textbooks and begin Plebe duties. It is a very busy time for your cadet, and it may be for you as well, as you prepare for a trip to West Point for Acceptance Day.

Count down, work out, hang on. Every day, every minute lived gets you that much closer to seeing that amazing young adult child of yours. Keep on keeping on. A-Day is coming!

CHAPTER 7
The Call
(when cadets want to quit)

Not every cadet will make it through Beast. For some, it's just not what they envisioned—and they want out. For others, it is a complicated mix of emotions. Some are not really sure what they want. It is not wrong to choose a different path when the one they are on ends up being wrong for them. There are thousands of reasons why cadets choose to leave. Athletes, experienced soldiers, military kids, and scholars, men and women, even those who've "always" wanted to be at West Point, may get there and find it is not what they'd expected.

If your cadet decides during Beast that West Point is not the right place to be, you will get "The Call." Not all Calls end in a cadet leaving; some have a change of heart. Three of our moms were kind enough to share the stories of their Calls. We are including their stories as examples, without any intention of representing any group. The experiences related here are just that—personal experiences—and we hope that reading about them might help you be better prepared to support your cadet through a similar situations, should it arise.

You May Not Quit

I dropped my son off at Beast and was devastated when the large mess hall doors slammed shut behind the parade at dusk that night. It seemed a chapter in my life was abruptly closing, but beyond those doors I knew my son's new chapter was just beginning. He had eaten, slept, and dreamed West Point for years. He had made the decision to delay starting college so he could attend the prep school that West Point required he attend before getting his spot with the class of 2013. I had no reason to believe that my intelligent, athletic, strong, and determined son would call me and say, "Mum, I'm coming home." However, six days after I left my son at Beast, he called.

It was ten o'clock on a Sunday night when the phone rang. My heart leapt as I saw the 845 area code flash across my caller ID. In a state of panic, I almost yelled, "Hello!" while thinking, "What's happened to my baby?!"

"Ma'am, this is the TAC officer. I am sitting here with your son and he would like to speak with you." In that instant every possible scenario flashed through my mind.

"Mum, I'm coming home. I've decided this isn't for me."

I was confused and in a state of disbelief. Still in shock, I replied, "What isn't for you?"

He continued, "This isn't the life I want; I'm signing my discharge papers now, I'll be out-processed, and I should be home by the end of the week."

To be honest, my heart took a momentary, joyful leap. My baby was coming home, thank God! As fast as joy filled my heart, though, reality filled my head. I can't tell you verbatim what I said, but I can tell you that I have never had such resolve or spoken to my son so sternly before—or since.

I clearly remember taking a deep breath and words just came to me. "Son, you may not quit." I continued, "You have worked too hard and wanted this too much to quit after six days. You may not quit."

Silence filled the air until he finally responded, "I'm 19 years old and I don't need your permission to leave."

There it was, the cold, hard truth: he didn't need my permission, and we both knew it. In that moment, hearing his voice quiver and listening to him tell me he was so tired and hungry and that he wanted to come home, all I wanted to say was, "I'll be right there, baby, you hold on!" But that isn't what came out of my mouth.

My son and I have what I think of as an atypical kind of bond. I often say we grew up together, as I had him when I was young and I was a single mom for most of his life. I've never had to discipline him harshly; he and I have been more like companions than mother and son. However, that night, in the strongest mother voice I could muster, I said, "You will not be quitting tonight. Do not sign that paper. Stand up from that table; go back to your barracks and go to sleep because you will finish Beast. You've worked too hard for me to let you make this decision from weakness. When you get to A-Day, then and only then will I allow you to quit; you will decide to leave from strength, not weakness. On A-Day, after you have finished Beast, if you still want to leave West Point it will be on your terms, and I will support you 100%. We will find another college and it won't be because you decided to quit; it will be because you chose to leave. There is a difference." Silence. I've heard that silence can be deafening, and believe me, that night it was.

My son said nothing but, "I have to go." He sounded

defeated. I had not given him the reaction he wanted or expected. I told him I loved him, and all he said was, "Bye," and the phone went dead.

That was, to date, the most difficult, tough-love thing I have ever had to do as a mom. It was the worst moment of my life. You can only imagine how distraught I was. I cried for hours; actually, I cried for days. Questions such as, "What did I do? What should I have said? Was I wrong?" filled my days and kept me awake every night for the next seven days.

What did I do next? I called in the troops—the mother troops (including my mother, of course). There is an army of West Point Moms on Facebook and someone always seems to be online day or night. Together, these women can battle any enemy that faces their children—and win. These selfless, strong women believe in "no woman left behind." My one panicked and fear-stricken post resulted in over fifty responses within an hour with words of advice, encouragement and guidance. These women circled me and became my lifelong friends that week. I didn't know if my son had resigned and left West Point or if he had stayed. I knew nothing. I wrote to my son and told him for the millionth time how proud I was of him. I shared news from home and sent clippings from *PEOPLE* magazine, cartoons and local current events. I called in backup and enlisted my family and friends to write letters or send cards, never mentioning quitting, only saying, "Hey, we're all still here." I sent letters with little goals I thought he could strive to meet, like: "Your ice cream social is a week away," or "Only __ days until March Back," etc.

Finally, eight days later (174 hours later; yes, I counted as I stared at the clock each night), I received a letter from my son. Feverishly, I ripped it open to find the most encouraging letter of the summer. It was filled with stories of the people he had met, interesting things he was learning, and questions about home. He was fine; there was no mention of the phone call or being unhappy. He and I never spoke another word that summer about quitting Beast.

One week before A-Day, I was prepared. I had contacted his second choice college after his initial phone call, sent in the deposit and registered him for classes. If he had decided to leave, I would be able to live up to my promise and he would not miss a beat. He would start college in September. I wrote to him and outlined his choices and assured him that I would support his decision now. I explained that successfully completing Beast meant that he would no longer be quitting West Point, but rather he would be choosing from strength to stay or to leave. He would have no regrets. I would happily bring him home after he felt the pride and accomplishment of having completed the toughest challenge he had ever faced in his 19 years.

I can tell you there was never a more beautiful sight than seeing my son walk towards me after the A-Day ceremony. He stood proud and accomplished; he was a man. There was no mention that day of the call from earlier in the summer until he and I were driving back from the hotel to West Point. I asked him if he wanted to continue at the Academy. I clearly remember his response, "Mom, I will talk about this once and never again. Thank you for not giving me a way out. There are good days and bad days, but this is where I'm meant to be. I'll always be glad you didn't let me quit." That was it—we have never discussed it again.

I handled The Call my way, which is not to say it should be the way you handle it for your child. To this day, three years later, I don't know if he realizes how tormented I was that summer: how I prayed, cried and questioned my response to his phone call. It was the longest summer of my life.

Do I think some cadets should come home when they decide to? Definitely! Please understand that I am not saying all cadets should stick it out. What I am saying is that no one knows your child better than you do. Be ready; know how you need to handle that dreaded phone call if it comes. I have heard of families who discuss before R-Day what the parents should say if the child calls, wanting to quit. That seems like a good idea to me. There is no shame in quitting and it takes nothing away from the honor of being appointed to the United States Military Academy. Army life is not for everyone, and living it for a while may be the only way for your cadet to find out if it is for him.

I Might as Well Get My Two Years

The phone call came on a Tuesday evening around 8:00 p.m. in early July. "Good evening, Ma'am. This is Major B____ at the United States Military Academy. Your son is here. Are you aware that he has resigned and is preparing to leave the Academy? Do you have any questions?"

WHAT?! I didn't know what to say; I could hardly breathe. I remember him handing my son the phone; I remember speaking to my son briefly; but I have no recollection of what was said. Then the conversation was over. My husband was at a meeting, but I called him anyway and told him he needed to come home right away.

We had received three letters from our son. The first one was really a downer: "I hate this; I don't think it is for me;

I am not sure what I am doing here." The second one was better: "The 4th of July concert was great; sorry about the first downer letter." The third one was back to questioning things. Then came the phone call. I didn't know what to do or who to talk to. Everyone on the online forums was talking about how great their letters were, that their sons and daughters were really making it through. How could my son be struggling?

My son initiated the conversation about West Point back in his junior year of high school. He sought out the coach to be recruited for his sport. He wanted this. What could have gone wrong? My husband and I were at a loss to figure it out.

Then we started thinking about his girlfriend and wondered if she was really being as supportive of him as he needed. We worried that she was filling his head with letters of "please come home to me." My husband placed a phone call to Major B_____ and asked him to "lose" the out-processing paperwork for a couple of days so that maybe we could sort this out.

We were able to communicate with our son a few times, but he was still convinced that he needed to quit. He was finally moved to transition barracks—where cadets are housed before officially leaving West Point. He had left his Beast company, and we were really concerned. I made one last phone call to him late at night, begging him at least to see this through to A-Day. "Don't quit in the middle of Beast!"

He said he would think about it, and then we waited to hear: was he going to be put on a plane home the next day, or would he go back? We didn't hear anything; we were on pins and needles every minute of every day. Then we got the Ice Cream Social phone call—he had decided to stay, but just until the end of Beast. We could take him home on A-Day, he said. We thought this was better than we had hoped.

We continued to write to him every day and offer up tons of encouragement, but we didn't receive another letter from him all summer. We had a very short third phone call, and he didn't say much. Then Beast was over; he called when he officially got his phone back during Reorgy week. Classes were about to start; he was going to start them, but he still wanted us to let him come home.

When we saw him on A-Day he was very somber and pretty miserable. He was not the happy-go-lucky boy he had always been. He just wanted to sleep and eat and be away from post. So that is what we did; it was a pretty awful weekend. But he stayed.

We convinced him that he needed to have a plan to transfer somewhere else and not just come home and sit. He worked very hard at figuring out where to transfer and how his semester at West Point would transfer. He also began to make a few friends and bond a little bit with the guys on his team. He was still unhappy, but maybe not every minute of every day. The entire first semester was rough; he was still determined to leave. Finally (thankfully?), his girlfriend broke up with him in late October. That was a turning point; without the negativity from her, his mood seemed to lighten a little. When he came home for Thanksgiving it was very hard to get him to go back. At Christmas time, we had more heart-to-heart discussions, and he realized that transferring an entire year of school was much better than just one semester, so he went back. Plus, the team was going to Puerto Rico over Christmas break, and he didn't want to miss that!

He still struggled during the second semester. He didn't

want to do any of the military training opportunities that the others were doing over the summer, so he signed up to take a class during STAP; that way he could get out of doing Airborne or Air Assault training, and he would have one more class to transfer. When he finally came home, we were still pretty sure that he wouldn't be returning for his Yearling year. He did invite a friend whom he had met at West Point to come and stay with us for a couple of days in June, and the two of them planned to return to Camp Buckner together. There was our hope: maybe our son would go as long as his friend was going back also. That is how it worked out. The friend was excited about going back to Buckner and it helped our son decide to give it one more try. He still talked about transferring, but now it was along the lines of, "I might as well get my two years in for free."

Finally, around November of Yearling year, the talk of transferring ended. Things had turned around and he realized that this was maybe not everything he had thought it would be, but it was giving him amazing opportunities and an education that was second to none. After getting his two years in for free, he committed and will graduate from West Point, just as he wanted back in high school.

As Prepared as She Knew How to Be

Your child, like mine, will have worked hard to prepare for the West Point Beast experience. For my child, that meant continuing team workouts, hiking in the approved Army boots (to break them in), wearing the black oxfords to walk to school and throughout the school day, maintaining upper body strength through push-ups and pull-ups, and trying to stay as healthy and fit as possible. There is not much that can be done to prepare for what the mental stress will be, other than reading about the experiences of others and imagining how to deal with various situations. Having done that as well, my child arrived as prepared as she knew how to be.

Jane was in a Beast squad with one other female cadet, which is typical. Unfortunately, the other woman dropped out of Beast early on. At that point, Jane found herself with no female companionship. Women who apply to West Point know that they are going into an environment that is dominated by males, and most have found ways to get a taste of that environment beforehand so that it is not a shock. Even those who are comfortable around "the guys" may be surprised, though, when there are suddenly no women to talk to at all!

Most squads have no more than two women assigned, so if one drops out early, the one remaining may find little to relate to in those few moments of downtime when her squad mates are talking about different ways to dump their girlfriends, or whatever the topic of conversation may have turned to. For those women who are recruited for Corps squad teams, there may be the benefit of some moments of time with other women during the time they spend with those teammates, but those women not on Corps squad teams (many of whom may be used to being on teams of female athletes) will certainly be dealing with some sense of isolation. Jane was definitely isolated.

To make matters worse, Jane developed foot issues. She developed horrible heel pain, which she described as sharp knives slicing through both heels. She knew the protocol: talk to her squad leader about her feet. However, Jane didn't want to be perceived as weak. She had been holding her own as the only female in her squad, but her feet were quickly becoming a serious problem.

Around this time, Jane was due her first phone call home. She called and said she wanted to quit; this was not the place for her. I encouraged her to stick it out, at least until the end of Beast. But Jane's feet were killing her! I urged her to tell someone, but she refused; she said that would be showing too much weakness. The call ended with Jane adamantly saying she was going to quit.

I asked for advice from more experienced parents and ended up contacting the Chaplain to make sure she got the message to seek medical treatment. I ended up hearing not only from the Chaplain, but from the TAC officer, who had contacted my child and determined that she was not mentally prepared and was no longer interested either in working toward becoming an officer or in completing the summer training. The TAC officer told me her pain was being treated, but that he had little doubt my child would begin out-processing soon. A few days later, he called to tell me it had begun.

Once the process was underway, I didn't hear from Jane again for a while. The TAC had explained that out-processing could take weeks, and that she would be counseled during that time to be sure that the decision to leave West Point was not being made hastily. It was about two weeks before I received another short phone call from her in which she told me she was still out-processing and had been required to turn in the mailbox key as soon as the process had begun. This was upsetting; I realized that for over two weeks, while I had been writing letters of encouragement, she had not received a one.

Out-processing takes a lot of time, but there is not much notice when it is over. A few weeks after the process had begun, I received a 7:30 a.m. phone call telling me to expect Jane home that evening.

Jane had been so gung-ho for West Point. She initiated all contact from the start. She required very little help or input in the application process. When she received her appointment, she was ecstatic. Even all her preparation and excitement were not quite enough to carry her through Beast, though. After leaving West Point, she found a better fit at a major university, where she is very happy.

These moms agree that it is a good idea to talk to your cadet before R-Day to be prepared for this possibility. There's a world of second-guessing between "Hang tough!" and "I'll be right there." Even if you didn't have that talk, and you're reading this during Beast, you can still spend a little time thinking about how you'll handle The Call if you receive it. You will be more confident and sure in your response if you've thought it out ahead of time.

At the end of the day, though, this is a decision your cadet must make. Trust yourself as a parent and advisor; trust your cadet to do what is best. If you do get The Call, realize that there are many who are willing and eager to help you through the aftershocks. The West Point Moms and West Point Dads Facebook groups, your local West Point Parents' Club, your Corps squad cadet's coach, the USMA Chaplain or someone in that office—all of these are willing to listen. If you want advice, there are many who have walked the path ahead of you, like the women who shared here, and they can offer wise counsel.

CHAPTER 8
Accepted at Last
(A-Day)

At long last, the summer draws to a close. A new class of cadets has passed through the gauntlet and emerged victorious over the Beast. Hooah! The Academic Year is about to begin: new company assignment, new roommate(s), new barracks, and lots of new books and new duties as well. Acceptance Day (A-Day) comes on a Saturday, after Reorgy.

Some parents, but not all, go to USMA for A-Day. Some parents choose A-Day over R-Day, if they can only attend one, because A-Day involves more time with the cadets and it represents the completion of a challenge rather than the start of one. It is a proud day for Corps, cadet, and parent alike when the Corps of Cadets accepts its next class.

If you go to A-Day, here are a few notes to help you know what to expect. Before the day, plan with your cadet where you will meet after the review. There are two statues on the edge of the Plain, and they make great meeting places. As you sit on the stands, the Eisenhower statue is to your left, and McArthur is to your right. When leaving the barracks, your cadet will be close to one of those statues and they make easy landmarks for meeting up.

On the day, remember to arrive at the gate early enough for security checks. It's another busy day, though not quite so busy as R-Day, but wait times may be long. You'll have to find parking on A-Day, too, and there won't be shuttles running as often as on R-Day. It's not a bad idea to be in place at the parade ground an hour or even two before the review begins, to be sure you have a seat where you want it. Take your sunscreen, sunglasses, water, binoculars, camera, phone, and a towel (to wipe the bleachers in case the morning dew has not evaporated yet).

The big event is a review—a parade—in which the New Cadets march out onto the Plain and form up into ranks, the Corps marches separately onto the Plain, and at a specific time the New Cadets march into place to join their companies in full formation. (Four years later, this process is reversed— the First Class cadets will march away from the Corps.) It is a moving sight, very patriotic, and symbolic of the historical importance of the United States Military Academy. The West Point band plays martial tunes; generals are present to review the cadets; an announcer explains the significance of the day. Guests are seated on stands to watch the pomp and ceremony and to look for their own particular Waldos. Companies line up A-I, 1-4, on The Plain, and parents line up in the bleachers A-I, 1-4; signs will be posted behind the bleachers so that you will have an idea where to sit for the best chance to see your cadet. If you sit on the left end of the bleachers, though, you'll be near the corner of the Plain, where the New Cadets make a gate turn and the ranks open up as the line moves right in front of the stands, making it easier for you to see faces. Also, each row of cadets is arranged by height. In general, the tallest cadets will be closer to the stands because they're on the outside of that turn and can take longer strides to keep lines even. Use this knowledge to judge where your cadet is likely to be in the row, based on relative height.

After you exit the stands from the review, sorry, but there's more waiting. The cadets have to return to quarters and complete various duties before they're released to come greet their families. This is usually not a very long wait. If you both have cell phones (after Beast, cell phone privileges are restored), you can wait in the shade of a tree or near the base of a statue until you get the call to go meet. Most companies don't require a lot from the Plebes on this day, but be prepared to wait, just in case your cadet has a few things to take care of. Hang in there. That next hug, when you see that cadet up close and personal, is going to be one of the best ever!

Your cadet may be on hyper-drive, overexcited to see you, but you may also notice a reserve, particularly on post. Plebes have to be very aware of themselves at all times to be sure they're not breaking a rule; this will likely be new for your son or daughter, and it may appear to you as uneasiness. Don't worry; once you get away from post, inside a private room, the reserve will most likely disappear. Of course, with that relief may come the need for sleep. Some parents report spending most of A-Day weekend watching their cadet sleep.

Also, there are rules about what's allowed and not allowed during A-Day weekend. It is a time to celebrate, and the Plebes do get some special privileges, but there are still restrictions about uniform and reporting in. Their commitment to USMA requires some limitations on their activities, even on this weekend. The rules change from year to year, but at this time, Plebes are not allowed to drink alcohol, even with parents, even in celebration, even if they are of legal age. Uniforms, including hats (cover) as appropriate, must be worn at all times that cadets are in public view; this means in restaurants, in vehicles, even in a hotel if they are outside of a private room. For this reason your cadet might want to order pizza and eat in the room, just for the freedom from uniforms! Many cadets send a long wish list home ahead of A-Day so the family arrives with the cadet's favorite comfy clothes and personal hygiene products. The cadet will want these items on Labor Day weekend when the first pass is typically taken, so the timing is perfect.

There are clearly set limits as to how far a cadet may go from campus on this weekend, too. The Academy has grown more generous in these limits over the years; accept whatever the limits are for your particular year and don't test them. Yes, there really are upperclassmen cadets and Academy personnel all around, and no, they're not all in uniform or on official patrol, but yes, they can still enforce disciplinary measures if a cadet is found violating USMA regulations, even off-post.

Lastly, there will be a time when your cadet needs to be returned to the barracks on A-Day. Alas, your cadet is not wholly yours at this point and must return to the barracks to sleep on Saturday night. Fortunately, you will also have most of Sunday with your cadet, if studies allow. The refrain returns here: Get to the gate early. Everyone will want to wait as late as possible, but the gate only lets through one or two cars at a time. Don't be the reason your cadet has to walk hours on a future date.

A final word about rules: The rules apply to your cadet,

and your cadet is responsible for knowing and obeying them. Don't stress over keeping up with all the details, but do check with your cadet before making plans, to be sure plans and regulations don't conflict. Trust what you are told, then, about the rules, and don't try to be "the mom" who keeps everyone in line. It's part of the letting go and acknowledging the adulthood of your child. Besides, if a rule is broken, your cadet is the one who bears the consequences, not you. This leads to a high level of motivation to know and obey those rules!

Enjoy your weekend. Celebrate the victorious end of the summer training. Give and receive as many hugs as possible. Listen until your ears are tired. Have a ball!

CHAPTER 9

The Longest Year
(Fourth Class citizenship, or Plebe year)

Your cadet has survived Beast, and so have you. Hopefully, you had a lovely visit at A-Day. If you were unable to attend, your cadet likely caught up on food and sleep and is ready to face the Academic Year head on! Having been accepted by the Corps, your New Cadet has become a Plebe—and just as in ancient Rome, this rank is just a little above that of slave. It would be an understatement, therefore, to say that Plebe year is challenging. It will probably be the toughest year your young adult child has experienced.

Plebes have a load of restrictions that only apply during the first year at West Point. There are specific places they may and may not walk, both indoors and out; certain paths and staircases (usually the simplest, most direct ones) are off-limits to Plebes. They must always have their hands "cupped" in a certain manner, in sort of a loose fist, when outdoors in public. They have to salute almost everyone on post; according to Bugle Notes, a handbook they must very nearly memorize, Plebes rank "the Superintendent's dog, the

Commandant's cat, the waiters in the Mess Hall, the Hell Cats (a West Point pep band), the Generals in the Air Force, and all the Admirals in the whole d****d Navy." That leaves a lot of people to salute, including roughly 3,000 cadets who outrank them and are happy to remind them of that fact. They can be stopped at any time and required to spout facts about obscure details of the geography and architecture of the Academy or the latest stock figures or sports scores. And all these people who require so much of them don't even address them by name; every last member of the Fourth Class of cadets is called "Plebe."

While the coursework and military training at West Point are rigorous, what many Plebes seem to struggle with most is time management. The Plebes have homework, projects, and class preparation, obviously. But they also have Plebe duties, which can include sorting and delivering laundry, removing trash, delivering newspapers, and calling minutes (announcing how much time is left before the next company formation— which means lining up for inspection or for moving out). On top of this, the Plebes have daily athletics time or Corps squad team practice. Most college students are used to some down time every day; Plebes often don't have this luxury.

The requirement to be excellent in every area puts a lot of pressure on every cadet. For some, the academics are a challenge, but not an unpleasant one; for some, the athletics are as much a release as a responsibility; and for some, the demands of military discipline and protocol suit their temperaments and understanding. For many, though, the opposite will be true: most will find a weakness in one area, whether it is academic, physical, or military, making this very full plate quite daunting.

If you are a mom who needs to be in constant contact with your offspring, you might want to step back and re-evaluate now. Are your needs adding additional pressure to your stressed-out Plebe? Are your long e-mails requiring extra time your Plebe doesn't have? (They get literally hundreds of e-mails every week.) Communicate with your child. Figure out together what your cadet is willing and able to handle in the way of communication from you during the Academic Year, and then respect that limit. Many weekends offer enough down time so that you and your cadet can catch up. As a mom, you don't want to add additional pressure to your cadet's life. Beware: mother is just one letter away from "smother."

Plebes get one pass per semester (although there are often opportunities to earn more—see "Leave and Passes"). Some cadets take their first pass on Labor Day weekend. After surviving Beast, Reorgy week and the first few weeks of classes, Plebes are quite eager to "get the heck out of Dodge." Some visit homes of new friends who live close by, others venture into New York City, and some get on a plane and come home.

Fall semester at West Point has a lot to offer your Plebe. Win or lose, football weekends are fun. Home games offer the opportunity to act like any other college student (sans beer). Parents can visit on game weekends for a chance to spend time with their cadet. Food is available both before and after games with company and team cookouts and Parents' Club tailgates. If you stay in a hotel within walking privileges, your Plebe can return there with you for some off-post family time.

West Point in the fall is a breathtaking sight. If you

can possibly get there during this season, do. For outdoor enthusiasts, the Appalachian Trail (AT) passes very close by the Academy. The October foliage on the AT is breathtaking. For those who prefer to drive and look, the view of New York City from the top of Bear Mountain in the clear autumn air is stunning. However, none of that is within walking privileges, so unless your Plebe saved a pass, you'll be going alone. Of course, the scenery right on campus along the Hudson is spectacular—they don't call it the Million-Dollar View for nothing.

When you chat with other West Point Moms during the first semester, the conversation invariably will turn to holiday travel. While many public school systems have moved to a longer Thanksgiving break, West Point is on the old-fashioned Thursday-Sunday break schedule. Your cadet will have a shortened day on the Wednesday prior to Thanksgiving, starting early and meeting all classes for shorter than usual times; leave begins after classes and all duties are completed. Your cadet should know an approximate time for departing for Thanksgiving break by early fall. Cadets can purchase bus tickets to nearby airports (available on campus from a bus company named GMK) and be home in time for turkey dinner. Cadets will be notified of times and locations for bus ticket sales, and the bus schedules will be posted on the USMA website once they are officially confirmed. For flight times, try to allow an hour to move from the GMK bus to the plane if the flight is departing from one of the larger airports in New York City. Of course, if your cadet is making the reservation, you don't need to be concerned about how long it takes a trained cadet with a few days' luggage to sprint through an airport and clear security in time to catch a flight.

At the end of any weekend, including leave times, cadets must return to barracks on Sunday by a pre-determined time (usually late afternoon or early evening). When it comes to arrival back on post, earlier is always better than later. Personally, I add fifteen to thirty minutes to my estimates of time needed for all the parts of the trip under my control when returning a cadet to West Point (packing car, getting gas, driving to airport, meeting girlfriend, parking, getting to security). That means I generally plan to leave my house roughly an hour earlier than I reasonably think I might leave on any other trip to the airport. On the return trip, be aware that sometimes the last GMK bus from the airport may arrive at West Point after the required time to report in. If you are the one purchasing airline tickets, allow LOTS of extra time for airline-related travel delays so that your cadet will be on an earlier bus and back in barracks in plenty of time for roll call.

"Plenty of time" is a relative term, we know, but being late is simply not an option for cadets, especially Plebes. We must include a note here particularly to West Coast moms: some parents decide it is not worth the expense of airfare to bring a cadet all the way home for Thanksgiving, because tickets are so expensive at this holiday. It is usually the priciest ticket of the year, regardless. Since it is also the busiest travel time of the year nationwide, adding in extra time to account for likely delays from the interstate all the way to the gate, with possible schedule changes in connecting airports, on top of the actual time in the air between New York and the West, leaves little time for a relaxed family holiday visit. Your cadet may not get home until some time on Thursday and may have to leave on Saturday night to be back to West Point on time. Some families choose instead to travel to New York themselves during Thanksgiving break (taking on the delays in their own more flexible schedules, allowing the cadet more down time during leave). Another option is to meet somewhere in the middle, but the logistics of that may be pretty stress-inducing, too. It may be that Thanksgiving break is not a time when you'll choose to see your cadet; you can be thankful, though, that any cadet who stays at West Point for the holiday has the option of being adopted by a local family or group to celebrate. (See "Missing Family Events," "A Home Away from Home," and "Adopt-a-Cadet" for more thoughts on this theme.)

Some have likened the Christmas season at West Point to the banquet at Hogwarts in *Harry Potter*. The week before finals (TEEs), the cadets have a special Christmas dinner. Designated Plebes are responsible for table decorations at this meal. If your Plebe has this task, you might receive a request for help during Thanksgiving break. Traditionally, the Plebes provide the upperclassmen at their tables with cigars after dinner. If your Plebe needs or wants your help with any of this, you'll be asked—otherwise, leave it alone. Your cadet can figure out where and what to buy just fine. After the dinner, you'll likely receive pictures of your darling child holding a lit cigar, possibly even smoking one—an image that might give rise to mixed feelings, but it is an important rite of passage at West Point. Try not to obsess about this; we know of no Cadets who have become chain smokers as a result of exposure to Christmas cigars.

TEE week is a stressful time for all cadets, just as exam week is at any college. Of course, Plebe duties still continue, so there's a bit more stress at West Point. There's not much we moms can do to help out, but we can send TEE boxes, care packages especially for this time. Check the "Boodle" chapter for some great ideas; "boodle" is West Point lingo for "goodies from home." Be sure to send extra, just in case your cadet's buddy doesn't have a mom like you!

The good folks at GMK offer buses for Christmas break travel to airports. Your cadet will receive notification when tickets are on sale. Winter travel in New York can get dicey. The weather is unpredictable and flight cancellations due to snow are common. For that matter, travel to the airport can be dicey. One year, a blizzard arrived as Christmas leave began, and the GMK buses took four hours rather than two to get to the (shutdown) airports. Your cadet should travel with a charged phone and charger. If your cadet is stranded in the city, there's nothing you can do, besides the obvious help to navigate the re-booking, if you're asked. If your Plebe gets stuck on the way home due to weather in your area, be assured that all you have to do is let the West Point Moms on Facebook know and a mom will be at that airport to bring your cadet to her home for a good meal, a warm bed, and a ride back to the airport the next day.

All too soon, Christmas break is over—especially if your cadet had a shortened one due to travel with a Corps squad team. The new semester begins with another Reorgy week. Cadets settle into new rooms with new roommates, purchase textbooks, and attend briefings. And then it begins: the Gloom.

"The Gloom" is the name for the long period from January to March, when the skies are gray, the snow is gray, the buildings are gray, the uniforms are gray, and spring break seems an eternity away. Is it any wonder everyone has a gray and gloomy mood? Cadets from similarly gray and cold climates are used to this, but those used to daily sunshine really do become depressed in this environment. As a mom, be encouraging, be cheery, and most of all, send fun boodle!

During the Gloom Period, moms are all abuzz with details and plans for Plebe Parent Weekend (PPW). This takes place the first weekend of spring break. Events are held on Friday and Saturday, and Plebes can depart sometime on Sunday morning. Since the advent of Facebook, moms have been getting to know each other online, so they have been scheduling some PPW time for a meet and greet. This typically takes place on Thursday evening prior to the official USMA goings on.

Some parents struggle with the concept of traveling to New York for a weekend, even a long one, only to turn around and go back home with their cadet. PPW is so much more than just time with your cadet, although by this point you know that every single minute with your cadet is precious, because those minutes are so few. It is a significant milestone for many Plebes, something that is uniquely theirs, a time when they can give you a glimpse of their world, whether to commiserate or to celebrate—or both. It is a way you can show your desire to understand that world and your support for your cadet. It's also your only opportunity for the "insider" tour of West Point until Firstie year. If there is any way you can get there, go.

What does the weekend entail? You will be permitted to go pretty much anywhere you want. There are guided tours of the uniform factory, dining hall, and in some years, the Superintendent's house. You'll have the opportunity to meet instructors who will tell you how wonderful your cadet is.

There are briefings, departmental demonstrations, open houses, barrack visits, and lunch in the mess hall. This is the weekend when many parents purchase their own cadet parkas. The best part of the weekend may be meeting cadets who have become friends with your own son or daughter. I remember telling my husband that I couldn't have picked out better friends for my son if he'd let me.

The Plebes are relaxed during PPW because the upper class cadets have left for their spring break, which started earlier in the day. (Even if their parents don't come to PPW, Plebes are not released until Sunday.) After a dinner on Friday with family and friends, don't be surprised if your cadet is anxious to return to the barracks for some fun with company mates. While the cats are away, the mice may want to play.

Saturday of PPW includes a parade. Since the upper class cadets are gone, Plebes are in charge of leading the Corps (well, at least the other Plebes). After the parade on Saturday morning, the TACs hold company open houses and briefings. If you have a great TAC like we did, there will even be a slide show where you can see some of what your cadet's company has been up to since A-Day. After this briefing, you'll be allowed to tour your cadet's barracks. For many moms, this is a view of the cleanest room the cadet has ever had!

If your cadet has developed a relationship with a sponsor family, you might be invited to drop by during PPW. Many of these families sponsor multiple cadets and hold an open house on this weekend so the cadets' families can stop by and meet them. It's good to put faces with the names of the people who are kind enough to be a home away from home for our cadets.

The big event of the weekend is the formal military banquet on Saturday night. Moms often fret about what to wear (see the chapter titled "What Not to Wear"), but you will really see a little bit of everything. The evening begins with the banquet in Washington Hall where you will sit with other members of your cadet's company. You'll have toasts, eat a lovely dinner (finished by an astonishingly delicious dessert!), and listen to an engaging speaker. The wine glasses at the banquet are engraved with the USMA crest and details about PPW. They become part of a set of commemorative glasses your cadet may collect over the course of the 47-month experience. If you bring your handy-dandy West Point tote that you picked up on R-Day, you can use it to stash your program, place cards, and wine glasses after the banquet. Trust us: you won't be the only woman in formalwear with a canvas tote; of course, you may ask your formally attired escort to carry it, too. Throw some bubble wrap or tube socks in there before the banquet so you will have something to wrap up the glasses.

After the banquet, the crowd will head over to Eisenhower Hall for the hop (West Point lingo for "dance"). It is a walkable distance, but expect it to take a while in heels, and be sure to have a wrap to protect you from the cold and wind coming off the Hudson. Shuttles may be available, especially if the weather is inclement. On arriving at Eisenhower Hall, you will go through a receiving line where your cadet will introduce you to various West Point leaders. Once you make it through the line, you can dance the night away with your cadet or your date, or you may find a nice quiet spot in Eisenhower to relax and visit. There are usually at least two ballrooms hopping with dancers and music—one a bit more sedate and formal (jazzy), one a bit more hip and happening (youthful). You will have the opportunity to pose for a formal portrait with Academy Photo, but that will mean standing in another long line. If that doesn't suit you, in addition to the formal portrait setting, there are plenty of nice spots in Eisenhower Hall to take your own family pictures.

Your cadet may or may not want to stay long at the dance. If your cadet has not invited a date to the evening's festivities, another upperclassman-free evening in the barracks might be more fun than hanging with the parents! Of course, you and your date may stay longer than your cadet, if you like. Enjoy your evening, even if it's a bit shorter than you'd hoped. Remember, it's not about you, Mom... it's about your cadet.

Depending on duties and schedules, your cadet will be released some time on Sunday morning. Some cadets head off on trip sections (trips sponsored by West Point) or vacations with friends. The lucky mom has her cadet home with her (or better yet, on vacation with her) for the rest of the week.

After Plebes return from spring break, it's all downhill until summer. Downhill doesn't mean there's no work, of course—not at West Point—but that the workload has built up momentum and may be a bit easier to carry. Once the sun starts showing up again, and with the end in sight, bearing up under the burden may also be a bit easier. The end of spring semester is an exciting time as Plebes find out what their summer assignments are, attend briefings, and get ready for TEEs. They have just about survived Plebe year!

Once the Plebes are done with TEEs, they sometimes get a few days off (called TEE leave) before they have to be back for parade drill for graduation week. A Plebe highlight during grad week is Recognition. The Plebes in each company form a line, and the other cadets in the company queue up (imagine the hand slapping after a little league game) and advance down the row of Plebes, introducing themselves by name. This is significant: upperclassmen will officially address your cadet by first name for the first time. Congratulations, Mom; your cadet has just been recognized.

Plebes are part of the graduation week activities. They are in the several parades, including the big one on Friday where the Firsties separate from the Corps (the opposite of what your Plebe did on A-Day) in preparation for graduation the next day. The Plebes also have various responsibilities during the graduation ceremony. Once those Firsties graduate, the Plebes are done: done with duties, done with the semester, and most of all, done with being a Plebe!

Hooray! You and your cadet have survived the toughest year at West Point. Everyone says the next year is so much better. If that's the case, why are the second-year cadets called "Yuks"?

CHAPTER 10
A Plebe No More
(Yearling—second year)

While being a Yearling (or Yuk) presents its own challenges, anything is better than being a Plebe! In general, after Plebe year, classes are harder and responsibilities are greater. However, Plebe duties and Plebe restrictions are gone. Greater freedom on the weekends, higher pay, and just not being a Plebe make for a better overall West Point experience!

During the second summer of this adventure called West Point, cadets complete Cadet Field Training (CFT). Much shorter than Beast, this is training in military skills needed in the field. Cadets often refer to this training as "Buckner" because it takes place entirely at Camp Buckner, where CBT concluded. CFT is an introduction to some of the major combat arms branches and combat tactics. It is meant to give cadets a very basic understanding of what the Army is about, so that when they lead soldiers, they will have some idea what those soldiers are experiencing in the field. Last summer was about learning to be a cadet; this summer is about learning to be a combat soldier. There is a closing ceremony, followed by a summer hop where cadets wear their India white uniforms for the first time. There is no March Back after CFT—there is a Run Back. Your cadet also may complete other military training before or after the weeks at Camp Buckner. Many specialized military programs offer training to cadets alongside active duty personnel, and your cadet may apply and be selected to participate in a wide variety of such programs, which may be conducted most anywhere there is a military post. Your cadet's summer schedule will not likely be the same as any other cadet's, as they all have different assignments and requirements to meet. In addition to military training, some cadets complete an academic course during the Summer Term Academic Program (STAP), and some participate in Individual Advanced Development (IAD) programs. STAP can be completed to make up for a course that was missed or failed during the Academic Year, or it can be a means to completing a degree program at a more manageable pace. IADs include Military, Physical, and Academic opportunities for short-term individual development, including specialized training in a sport and programs similar to internships.

A Yuk's first chance at leadership within the Chain of Command comes after the Plebes return from March Back and join their Academic Year companies. Each Yearling cadet is assigned to supervise one or two Plebes as a Team Leader. A lucky Yuk gets a "squared away" Plebe—one who masters the system easily and follows orders without incident. Otherwise, the Plebe cuts into the Yuk's personal time. This is especially true if the Yuk is assigned a "superstar"—a Plebe who seems not to "get" how things work, who seems almost to draw negative attention by being on the edge of what is accepted and expected of Plebes. If that's the case, your Yuk might be in for a long term! Not to worry—this is the stuff of great stories on visits home, and the assignments only last for one semester. Second semester Reorgy week in January brings a new team to lead, along with the chance for a better experience than first semester.

During Yearling year, cadets declare their majors. The Dean has briefings on this and instructors give counsel to cadets as well. Sometimes cadets will even solicit advice from their parents! Every cadet at West Point must choose a field of engineering for a primary focus, and an academic major to complete alongside the engineering track. Some have their goals set and make major choices based on what they will do after the Army, while others choose majors based on what they want to do in the Army. When my son was choosing his major, the Dean said, "Study what you like, as you already have a job waiting: Second Lieutenant." Plebe year for my son had involved a ride in a Blackhawk helicopter, and he had his heart set on learning to fly one. Aviation is a very desirable branch assignment, and branch choice is based on class rank. My son therefore chose his major based on what he thought he could excel in, so he could rank high enough to branch aviation. He is now in pilot training in Fort Rucker. Perhaps one day he'll be able to use that German major!

Yuks are allowed OPPs (Off-Post Privileges). This means they are authorized to travel in a much wider area than Plebes are, as much as 75 miles from campus. A Yuk can go someplace where there's actually something to do! Yearling cadets can go into New York City for a day or an evening, head to the mall for a movie, or run over to Central Valley and eat at a favorite restaurant. West Point weekends begin to feel a little bit more like civilian college weekends, though cadets are still required to be in barracks by a designated time each night unless they've taken a pass.

The Yuks have a dance in January called Yearling Winter Weekend. Many invite dates from home, while some have dates set up by cadet friends. In typical West Point fashion, there is a banquet and then a hop. Very few parents are invited to this event; it is for the cadets. Many cadets take a pass after the hop and head into the city for some fun.

Second semester Yuk year, the cadets will hear about their summer leadership opportunities. After being Team Leaders all year, they will spend the summer in some sort of leadership detail. Some will be leaders at Summer Leadership Seminar, a program to introduce high school students to USMA; others may be involved in some aspect of Beast. Occasionally, other factors require cadets to put leadership off until the next summer, but eventually they will have a leadership detail.

Having survived Plebe year, moms usually find Yuk year to be much easier. Knowing a bit more about the routines, the language, and the challenges makes us better able to face new situations as they arise, and there are simply fewer new situations. Almost everything was new and different last year; this year most things are routine. More and more, your cadet will be making decisions without consulting you, which is as it should be. Once again, West Point is helping your child become an adult in a way that doesn't happen as a rule at other colleges. Enjoy your developing adult relationship; and when this year is over, you'll be halfway through your 47-month adventure.

CHAPTER 11

'Til the Cows Come Home
(Second Class, third year)

When the third year of West Point begins, the cadets are known as "Cows." This term originates from the 1800s, when after the summer furloughs the cadets returned much larger, due to more plentiful food at home than at the Academy. Some would say that particular distinction, with regard to the food, persists today. While the name carries different connotations in modern culture, third-year (Second Class) cadets are proud of their hard-earned rank and don't seem to mind being called Cows.

During fall term Reorganization week, the Cows have a briefing where they reaffirm their commitment to the Army (called Affirmation Night or the Affirmation Ceremony). Sorry, moms, you are not invited to this event. If you are lucky, your cadet will take a picture or two for you. At the briefing, cadets basically sign again the paperwork that they signed on R-Day. This obligates them to finish at the Academy and serve for five years of active and three years of reserve duty in the Army. Technically, they are not committed to serve until they cross the threshold into their first class of the fall semester. After that, if they choose to leave, they will owe military service or money to repay the Army for their time at USMA. This leads to an unusual phenomenon on the first day of the Academic Year when many members of the Cow class hesitate in the hallways until the last moment before the beginning of class, watching and encouraging one another to step off into the next ten years of Army life. Some Cows get cold "hooves" (feet) and do not step off on this morning; some of them actually move to Transient Barracks to consider for a few more days. Of course, their buddies go by to check on them and help them make the decision. It is not a move to make lightly; if your Cow has some second thoughts, you may not even know about it, but if you do know, realize that it's quite normal. Promising at age twenty to do something for ten years? That's a big deal.

At the end of their Yearling year, the Cows were most likely scrambled (moved to new companies). The timing and number of class scrambles gets adjusted periodically. You don't need to know when or how often it happens, but expect to hear some talk about it, either pro or con. If the Cows have been scrambled, your cadet will begin the year getting to know a whole new group of cadets. The first few weeks or months might be awkward, but eventually new bonds are formed and cadets expand their circle of friends. It's good preparation for Army life, where people are continually transferring in or out, and where assignments don't usually last more than a few years.

Classes, while still challenging, are potentially more interesting as some of them relate to the cadets' majors. After four grueling semesters of required courses, Cows are finally to the point where they have some choice in what subjects they take. Class loads are intense, and coupled with increased demands as Cows take on more and more leadership for the Corps of Cadets, you may find you have a very busy (and perhaps stressed-out) cadet.

Cows have a year of milestones ahead. They order their class rings, receive their Cow loans (read: large sum of money, low interest rate), and get to bring their cars on post. All of these are moves toward the future when cadets will be graduates starting life as Second Lieutenants. Ordering the class ring may take place outside your awareness, but cadets have the option of ordering miniature rings or pendants for girlfriends or mothers. If your cadet chooses to order a pendant for you, you might be consulted about options you would like.

Cadets can usually bring cars to West Point after spring break in March (occasionally this date is changed based on the performance of the football team or some other major Corps accomplishment). Some cadets have a car all ready to bring back, and others shop over Christmas or spring break. No matter what you may hear, "everyone" does not have a car on post any more than "everyone" was doing any other given activity when your child was growing up. But for those who do bring a car, they certainly enjoy their newfound weekend freedom.

In the winter, Cows have a special party called 500th Night, where they celebrate having 500 days until their graduation. Like Yearling Winter Weekend, this is not a family event. It's amazing to see how organized the cadets become at planning their social events. They rent houses, make travel plans, figure out the food… and make sure that everyone has a date. The cadets who know students attending schools close to West Point are great about setting up their friends who have no "special someone" to bring from home.

After Cow year, the summer training is usually very relevant to the branch in which your cadet hopes to serve. If this didn't happen after Yearling year, this is the time for Cadet Troop Leader Training (CTLT), when your cadet will shadow an active-duty officer, hopefully in the branch your cadet wants to select. Some cadets get to do CTLT in a foreign country, which makes it a bit more exciting. Others are assigned to posts around the United States. My cadet was sent to Fort Campbell, Kentucky, where he followed an aviation officer. Seeing the day-to-day life of the officer with his unit convinced my son that aviation was the right branch for him. Some cadets, though, will totally rethink their branching goals after CTLT. The experience in a branch they supposed would be a good fit may not be so good in reality. This kind of training helps cadets to learn that fact before a commitment has been made to a specific branch.

Hopefully, this is the summer when cadets will figure out what they want to do in the "real" Army. When summer training ends, the cadets return to West Point to finish their final year of Academy training. At long last they are Firsties!

CHAPTER 12
Top of the Food Chain
(Firstie year)

As a teary-eyed parent on R-Day, nothing seemed so far away as Firstie year. As any cadet will tell you, however, the days are long, but the years are short. The final year will be upon you before you know it.

The first major event in the year of a First Class cadet is Ring Weekend. This is a big parents' weekend. Obviously, everyone doesn't attend, but if you can get to Ring Weekend, it will be worth it. The weekend begins with the ceremony awarding cadets their class rings. This is held at Trophy Point on the Friday afternoon of Ring Weekend. Parents and guests scatter on the lawn, sitting on blankets, watching as Firstie cadets march in by companies. After some speeches and words of commendation, cadets receive their much-anticipated rings. Many pictures follow. Like late summer most anywhere, the weather is unpredictable, so be prepared for hot sun or heavy rain. Our year, we made a mad dash to the library as the bottom fell out of the sky.

After the Ring Ceremony, cadets and families generally go out for a nice meal. Some cadets will have arranged for dinner with a large group, while others prefer to be with just family. For example, my son and his friends made reservations and selected a "prix fixe" menu at a local restaurant. We dined with his closest friends and their families. Seeing the new rings and hearing talk of future plans highlighted the weekend for me. The cadets rented a house for the weekend, so after dinner they ditched the parents. We knew it would be a long night for our cadet, so we made no breakfast or lunch plans with him. Some parents took advantage of free time the next day to see sights in the area or shop at local outlets.

Saturday evening of Ring Weekend is set aside for more pictures, a banquet, and a hop. August in New York can be absolutely ghastly. The men generally swelter in their suits and tuxedos, while the moms can be much more comfortable in their cocktail dresses. The Ring Weekend hop in our year was probably typical—mostly parents and very few cadets. My cadet and his group were anxious to get back to the house they had rented. Walking into the hop, he asked me about how long I'd like to stay. I told him he could take off any time he wanted: after three years, I had my own West Point friends—thank you very much. He left soon afterward for his own celebration, and my husband and I had a lovely time without him. We were able to catch up with friends we had met at USMA events over the course of the previous three years. The moms enjoyed showing off their new West Point jewelry. The cadets traditionally give their moms a replica of their class ring, in the form of a pendant or mini-ring. We call this the "mom trophy." It's hard work being a West Point Mom! We deserve a trophy!

Sometime before the end of the first semester, Firsties have a big event called "Branch Night," where they learn which branch of the Army they will be serving in over the foreseeable future. Firsties gather in Ike Hall and sit by company. Their TACs hand out envelopes with branch information, and on a given signal, all cadets open their envelopes. For Firsties, this is the culmination of over three years of hard work. Obviously everyone cannot get his first choice, and it's likely some will be disappointed in the results. Those cadets will make the best of the situation and move forward. In fact, Army studies show that there is virtually no difference in job satisfaction after two years in a branch assignment, regardless of whether the branch was a first choice or a lower one. No matter the results, much celebrating ensues afterwards at the Firstie Club.

A bright spot in the middle of the Gloom Period is Post Night, when the Firsties choose where they will go after graduation (and after their initial Army training). Cadets gather with everyone who has selected the same branch. Signs are displayed around the room with paper soldiers attached, denoting how many spaces are available at each particular post. The cadets choose posts one at a time, based on their order of merit. Once the paper soldiers on a sign are gone, that particular post is closed. Again, this is a night that can have great celebrations or great disappointments. Like Branch Night, this night leads to revelry at the Firstie Club.

What the cadets don't know about Post Night is the whole behind-the-scenes West Point Mom connection. While they are sitting, waiting to pluck their paper soldiers, the moms are on Facebook chatting about where their cadets might land. The waiting is maddening! Slowly, one by one, the moms pop up to share the big news of where their respective cadets will spend the next three years. For the moms, this is an emotional day. While there's no Firstie Mom Club for celebrating or commiserating, there is Facebook chat and a glass of wine.

The next major event for Firsties is 100th Night, the celebration of 100 days until graduation. Most parents do not attend this event, although there are always a few who are invited. The cadets wear civilian dress clothes and usually invite dates for the weekend. The event begins with a satirical play lampooning their four years at West Point. Afterwards, the cadets enjoy a cocktail party and a banquet. Again, many rent houses or spend the weekend in New York City.

After 100th Night, the Firsties, along with the rest of the Corps, begin the countdown to graduation. As the time grows shorter, announcements and jokes refer to "how short the First Class is." Classes, duties, and physical training continue. The APFT must be passed one last time. TEEs must be endured once more. With jobs already waiting for them, though, the Firsties can finally see some of the advantages of a West Point education over even the best education at a civilian college. In uncertain economic times, guaranteed employment is a huge boon. Of course, Firsties also face uncertainties not common to their civilian counterparts, since the guaranteed job involves possible (likely) service in a war zone. Know all this and ponder it in your heart; your Firstie will confide in you if it seems appropriate, and you can always confide in the West Point Moms to get your support.

Different from civilian colleges from beginning to end, West Point holds a multi-day celebration for graduation. Parents and other guests may attend various receptions, awards ceremonies, choral concerts, baccalaureate services, multiple parades, and a banquet before the main event on Saturday morning and commissioning later in the day. (For tips on dressing for all these events, see "What Not to Wear.") The graduation speaker is generally a very high-ranking government official—the President, Vice President, Secretary of Defense, and Secretary of the Army, among others, have all spoken at USMA graduations. Of course, you might be interested less in the pomp and more in the circumstance that your cadet is about to join the Long Gray Line of graduates from the United States Military, a line extending more than two hundred years back in time.

This day may mark the end of your cadet's time at West Point, but it signifies just the very beginning of your Second Lieutenant's Army career. The 47-month adventure is over, but many new adventures await you both.

CHAPTER 13
"Oh, You _Have_ to..."
(what everyone says you must do, see, buy)

No, you don't.

You're going to hear that phrase, "Oh, you _have_ to..." from different people at different times during your 47-month adventure, and it will be stated with great conviction. Some of these people will be more experienced West Point parents, whose counsel you respect. Some will be friends and family who want what is best for you. "You have to go to..." "You have to buy..." "You have to keep..." However, what you really have to do is say to yourself, "No, I don't."

You can drive yourself to the nuthouse or the poorhouse trying to keep up with all the swag available for West Point parents. Bumper stickers, license plates, license plate frames, window decals, T-shirts, sweatshirts, hoodies, golf shirts, stuffed animals, pompoms, tie tacks, suspenders— if it has a surface, someone has probably tried to write or embroider "West Point" or "Army" on it. You can't possibly have them all, and really, you don't have to have any. Your son or daughter can be absolutely successful in pursuit of an academic degree and a military commission completely without regard to how much memorabilia you collect. Also, you will be proud of that accomplishment and have plenty of memories without a bunch of stuff to wash or dust or preserve to "help" you remember.

The same is true for USMA events. Being from Georgia, where football is a religion, we've learned that the Army-Navy game is a big deal for West Point (and Annapolis) parents around here. They like to go together to the game, get a block of rooms, plan a cocktail party the night before, etc. But a cadet can go through the entire 47 months without meeting parents at an Army-Navy game, and parents can make it through that same period without the experience, too. As far as we know, that can happen without permanent emotional scarring for either party, as well. R-Day, A-Day, Plebe Parent Weekend, Ring Weekend, even graduation, are all events worth attending, but time and money and other obligations simply don't allow everyone to attend everything.

Find where you're comfortable, emotionally and financially, and what helps you (and your cadet) get through your personal 47-month experience. Attend or buy or keep what helps with that, and don't think twice about all that other stuff that other people have to have or do. Don't accept their standards as your own, and remember that what is important to you is what got you where you are today: You're a West Point Mom! You rock! So be yourself.

CHAPTER 14
What Not to Wear
(dressing for West Point events)

As I write this, I am still on my post-Ring Weekend high. Ring Weekend was by far the best weekend I've ever spent at West Point. I think the reason for that is because at this point I'm comfortable and know what to expect. I know where places are, I know people, and I know what to wear.

Over the years I've seen moms get so stressed over what to wear to West Point events. There are two extremes in response to this question. First, there are the pseudo-military protocol purists who believe "casual" means men in a blazer and ladies in a skirt or dress with stockings. On the other end of the spectrum is the "anything goes" crowd. Their mantra is "no one will say anything to you; wear what you want."

They're both right—sort of. The first group, while overdressed, perspiring and miserable, is correct in that conservative attire is always appropriate. However, no one expects anyone to walk up and down hills in hose and heels. Parents need to be comfortably dressed for both the occasion and the required walking. Men in khakis and polo shirts and women in sundresses or capris will be plenty dressy for warm weather events. For outdoor events such as R-Day and A-Day, you are absolutely fine in capris, longer shorts and casual skirts. Leave the heels for evening wear at formal events. Comfy flats are the correct West Point Mom shoes. (Yes, this includes tennies on weekends, like PPW, that include lots of walking).

Just as there are those who will always overdress, there are those who won't wear enough. Somehow, the man in the blue "wife beater" undershirt found his way into several of my pictures. With him in the crowd were several "hoochie mammas." Seriously, ladies: cover up "the girls" while at West Point. Shorts, skirts and dresses need to be fingertip length or longer, and fleshy exposures need to be kept at a minimum. This goes for sisters and girlfriends, too.

Some moms want more specificity when it comes to what to wear at each event, so we offer the following:

- **R-Day** is going to be hot. Be comfortable. Shorts are fine if they are not too short. You will see women in sundresses, casual skirts, capris, and skorts. You will see many women dressed inappropriately; don't be one of them. You will do so much walking this day. If you wear sandals, make sure they are comfortable. Do yourself a favor and do not wear any kind of heel at all.

- **A-Day** will be a bit hotter and more humid than R-Day. Light, breathable fabrics are the key to comfort. You won't be walking nearly as much as R-Day, but you still will have a decent hike from where you parked to the parade field. After the parade you will be walking to wherever your cadet wants to meet. Again, go for comfy shoes.

- **PPW** is the formal event in March of Plebe year. Formal dresses can be long or short; it really doesn't matter—you will see a good mix of both. You'll see women who are in church dresses, and you'll see full-length sequined gowns. Here's another good reason to join the West Point Moms on Facebook: volunteers maintain Cinderella's Closet, a listing of formal dresses that members are willing to donate for use at West Point events. Of course, local consignment shops are another source for great prices on formalwear. A tight budget doesn't have to stand in the way of your looking gorgeous at Plebe Parent Weekend or any of the other formal events during your 47-month adventure. Bear in mind it is cold in New York in March. If you wear a long gown you can wear full length Spanx, which act as long underwear in protecting you from the frigid breeze off the Hudson. Remind the sisters and girlfriends that modest gowns are appropriate at West Point functions. Few young ladies can wear a strapless dress without adjusting it all night. It might be a good idea to save the strapless gowns for another day. During the PPW daytime events, warm casual clothing is appropriate. Khakis, corduroy pants, and nice jeans are all fine. A "West Point Mom" hoodie is always an appropriate garment. Many parents purchase cadet parkas early on Friday of PPW and show them off the rest of the weekend.

- **YWW** is an event for Yearlings. Very, very few parents are invited to this event. If you are asked to attend, the same dress applies as for PPW.

- **500th Night**. Again, this celebration during Cow year

is not a parent event. On the very remote chance you are invited, the same dress applies as for PPW.

- **Ring Weekend** is in August of Firstie year. This weekend is to celebrate the First Class cadets who are receiving their class rings. The Ring Ceremony is at Trophy Point. Parents sit on blankets on the hill overlooking the area. If you're in a dress, it needs to be long enough that you can sit on the ground and be decent. You'll see the moms mostly in sundresses and skirts. Most of the dads are in shorts and polo shirts. Saturday there is a banquet and a hop. It's a great weekend to be a woman and be able to get away with a sleeveless dress. The men absolutely roasted in their suits and tuxes in Washington Hall (no air conditioning). Most women will be in short cocktail dresses. Think "festive party." The banquet is on Saturday evening, but in late afternoon, when the sun is its warmest, you'll likely be at Trophy Point posing for pictures with your cadet. You'll want to have two pairs of shoes: one for the banquet and one for walking around in. Fortunately it starts cooling off a bit after the banquet, and the hop is at Ike Hall, where there is air conditioning.

- **100th Night**. This is a Firstie celebration that may include dates but rarely includes parents. If you are invited, dress as for PPW.

- **Graduation Week**. There are so many events this week. Men need to be in khaki pants and polos for most events and ladies can be in sundresses, skirts, and capris. Leave the pantyhose at home, as you will swelter in them. You'll need a nice sundress if you attend the Superintendent's reception (a short "How do you do?" in his garden or in Ike Hall). The Graduation Banquet is on Friday night. This is a formal event. If your hubs got a tux for PPW and/or Ring Weekend, he can drag it out again. This is your last chance to look amazing during your 47-month adventure. Elegant is the key word for the Graduation Banquet. You'll see both long and short dresses, but mostly short, as May is a hot month at West Point. You could probably get away with the same dress you wore to Ring Weekend, but don't forget to check the West Point Moms' Cinderella's Closet if you'd like to try a new gown. For the actual graduation ceremony, you will be sitting out in the heat for hours and hours (hopefully the heat and not the rain). Wear a lovely sundress with a great hat. Don't forget the dark sunglasses; not only will they protect your eyes, but they will hide the tears you know are bound to show up as you watch your cadet on the big day.

That's pretty much it. Graduation brings an end to your concerns about what to wear to West Point. Of course, as an Army mom, you may have more special military events in your future, but your West Point Mom training will serve you well. You'll always know what not to wear.

CHAPTER 15

Academic Survival
(maintaining grades)

Most of the cadets at West Point came from being the "big fish in the small pond." They were tops in their high schools and communities in academia, sports and leadership. Upon arrival at West Point (big pond), they became very little fish. With the start of the Academic Year, they became little fish who work very hard!

When my oldest started college at our state university, his advisor strongly encouraged his advisees to take only 14 credit hours at a time... he didn't want students to "overdo it." I wondered how long it would take to graduate at that rate. (Now I know: 4½ years, including one summer session.) On R-Day at West Point, the Superintendent's briefing showed me that my second son would take between 18 and 21 hours each semester; he'd be done in 47 months. In addition to the 18+ hours, cadets have mandatory duties, formations, athletics and training.

In some weeks cadets are given more assignments than they can possibly adequately prepare. Cadets refer to these as "Thayer Weeks," after Colonel Sylvanus Thayer,

Superintendent of USMA from 1817 to 1833, who developed the academic system still used at the Academy today. Thayer emphasized self-study, daily homework, and small class size; the cadets blame him for weeks when the small class size keeps them from hiding from the consequences of insufficient study and homework—Thayer Weeks. Every cadet "recites" in every class, every day. There's no slumping down in the seat and hoping not to be noticed. That's a constant result of Thayer's system. But his name is invoked when several classes have tests or projects or papers due during one week. That happens in other schools, of course, but like so much about West Point, there's a special name for it here. These weeks, which occur incidentally and not by design, are not the times for you to expect long chats with your cadet. While this academic overload is going on, realize that company duties haven't changed. Team practices, likewise, are continuing. If your cadet is on a Corps squad team, practices are just as intense during Thayer weeks as during other weeks; in fact, some cadets have to take work along as the team travels (or even turn it in early). The point is that cadets are very busy in and out of class.

You aren't going to see grades or progress reports unless your cadet authorizes them. You will only know what your cadet tells you. If your cadet is struggling, please offer encouragement to get help ASAP. "I thought I could pull it out," is all too often heard after academic separation. Chain of Command, professors, and friends want to help your cadet. If your cadet mentions poor grades, it is not helicoptering to suggest getting help (okay, maybe it is a little, but still do it).

The Center for Enhanced Performance is an Academy department specifically dedicated to assisting cadets to develop the skills necessary to succeed in academics and in general. There are other resources available as well, as highlighted in this story from one of our West Point Moms about her cadet's journey through academic difficulty.

Additional Instruction

AI stands for "additional instruction," as in tutoring. I learned this last summer. Our Cow came home for two weeks' leave and brought with him a cadet friend. Together they gave a presentation to five potential future cadets. I learned more then about his successes and struggles in his first two years at West Point.

He said that when he arrived at West Point, one of the things that stuck with him was the Commandant's speech in which he said, "West Point is a hard place to be at, but it is a great place to be from! You've worked hard to get here, and our goal is to help you stay here. Help is available here 24/7. You need to ask and go get the help you need, then do the work, if you want to stay here. We want you to succeed!"

My cadet found himself in Plebe year, at six weeks into the fall term, getting an "F" in two classes. He told us that maybe this was not the place for him, after all. We listened and encouraged him to get help and to finish the semester, and we asked him not to consider quitting at that point. We also assured him that it was not our pride that we were worried about, but our son. If he quit now, in a few years, would he look back with regret that he did not stick with it long enough or try all the help that was available to him?

I was so proud of him when he said to the future cadets that for one of the subjects, he took over 30 hours of AI. I thought that was a lot of free time and weekends given up for AI. He said later in his presentation, "If you want to stay at West Point, there are ways. You need to work hard, but the help is there." My son said AI helped him to build relationships with some teachers that now knew him very well. He started loving history and his history teacher. It was one of classes he had been failing, but it was his favorite subject by the end of the semester. He managed to earn a B- in that class. We met his teacher at PPW, and he said very nice things about our son.

Just as in any other academic program, the key at USMA is to seek help when you think you don't understand something, not to wait until you are too far behind and the grades are hopeless. Encourage your cadet to get online and sign up for AI slots with someone: a teacher, a classmate, or an older cadet. One Firstie who helped my son reserved a library room, brought an energy drink, and did an exam practice with my cadet for three hours. He checked his progress every day. That's dedication on the Firstie's part.

It was a semester-by-semester struggle for the first two years for my cadet. After that, something snapped into place, and now he is just running with it.

Classes, grading, and ranking at West Point can be confusing. If you are an information junkie, you can read more about it on the Dean's webpage (www.westpoint.edu/ academics). All you really need to know is that your cadet is graded on academic, military, and physical programs. Grades in these three areas are combined and calculated to determine your cadet's class rank. Class rank will be a factor in both branching and posting choices during Firstie year. No matter how you look at it, it's a heavy load and sometimes cadets are going to struggle. If or when you see this happen, it's fine to remind your cadet that help is available.

No matter what your cadet's siblings say, West Point is harder than a civilian college. There are more classes and more requirements to juggle. What can we moms do? Not much; just be that encouraging voice they need to hear, or be the listener when they need to blow off steam. Get used to hearing, "This place sucks," because sometimes it just does.

CHAPTER 16

Separation

(leaving USMA at the request of the Academy)

When your child goes to college, the plan is usually to enter and complete a four-year course of study. The institution where this journey begins may turn out not to suit the student's tastes, abilities, or interests, and if the unsuitability is significant, a change of course might be in order—even a transfer to another school. Likewise, the institution may determine that the student is not a good match for its goals, standards, or emphases, and that may lead to a change in course. In some instances, the course might be interrupted for a period of months or even years; alternatively, it might be extended for any number of reasons and the desired four-year degree might take much longer than four years to achieve. All of this is considered normal and it is nothing to be alarmed about; it is part of the process of finding one's way into the adult world.

When your child goes to the United States Military Academy, however, things are a bit different. A USMA Cadet Candidate intends to enter and complete a four-year course of study; officially, according to the letter offering the appointment, that is a "47-month experience." If, during the 47 months, a cadet perceives a need or desire to take a break, take a term off, try something different—sorry, no such luck; 47 months means 47 continuous months, and there are very few exceptions to that schedule. If, during the first half of those 47 months, the cadet finds that the Academy does not suit his or her tastes, abilities, or interests, a decision may indeed be made to finish the course elsewhere or to change course entirely. If at any point during the 47-month experience the Academy determines that the cadet is not suitably meeting its requirements, there will definitely be a change in course, and it will be made as an offer the cadet can't refuse.

At a civilian school, this would be known as a decision to withdraw from a program, or a transfer. This sounds peaceful enough, like a simple shift in position. At West Point, it is called "separation from the Academy." The words themselves imply an unpleasantness, a pulling apart of things that are bound together. Indeed, beginning in the shared trials of Beast Barracks, your cadet has been more and more tightly bound to other cadets and to the Academy, and separation from the Academy is physically, socially, psychologically, and spiritually wrenching. It is much more than a shift in position and much more challenging than voluntary withdrawal from a civilian college.

Separation can result from a variety of circumstances, all of which have in common a failure to meet USMA standards in a particular area. If a cadet is injured and unable to continue duties, if a cadet does not meet the Army Physical Fitness Test (APFT) requirements, if a cadet violates the honor code, or if a cadet does not maintain a specific academic Quality Point

Average (QPA), separation can result. Cadets know this from the outset, and your cadet will most likely know more than one person who is separated from the Academy. The details of separation vary, and because cadets are constantly graded on all aspects of their fitness to continue in the Corps, every case will be unique. Here's what moms need to understand about the various kinds of separation.

Physical fitness standards are quite high at USMA, and if your cadet becomes seriously ill or injured it will be difficult or impossible to continue to meet those standards. If this is the case, Chain of Command will intervene to help as much as possible, working in tandem with the medical staff of the Academy to be sure the illness or injury is treated appropriately. If your cadet is faced with this sort of challenge, and if the condition does not improve, he or she may be excused from duties and sent home on medical leave to recuperate and regain strength. However, re-admission after such a leave is not a guarantee; it will still be necessary for the Academy to evaluate the cadet's readiness to return to duties, and a medical leave may end with separation.

Separation can also come even without an injury, if a cadet is not able to perform up to USMA standards on the APFT. These tests are administered periodically during the 47 months, and a failure to meet standard means extra work and supervision to get the weak area strengthened so as to meet requirements. This is a chance to work together with a buddy to improve performance; most cadets are more proficient in one area than another, and "cooperate to graduate" is a slogan that encourages them to share their strengths with others who are struggling so that the team comes along at its best. Often this cooperation works as a trade, where one is more scholarly and another is more athletic, for example, and the two help develop each other's weak areas while exercising their respective strengths. Even with such help, though, and even when a cadet is doing his or her best, not all bodies are made to do what West Point requires bodies to do. Continually falling short of the standard is grounds for separation from the Academy.

There is an honor code at West Point: "A cadet will not lie, cheat, steal, or tolerate those who do." You will hear of people violating this; complaints of rule-breaking are common in any group, as is genuine rule-breaking. However, the code is real, and a cadet can be separated from the Academy for violating it. Plagiarism falls under this heading, along with cheating on tests or research. Most papers turned in at the Academy require cadets to sign a page stating that they received no assistance on the writing of the paper; of course this does not include tutoring or instructional help, but the school is serious about cadets doing their own work and standing or falling based on their own efforts. In the big picture, this is what we want. Our Army officers have lives in their care, and they must be able to think and communicate clearly in order to protect life and property in service to our nation. Education is not about making good grades, but about becoming educated. The honesty required by the Honor Code also allows cadets to live in an atmosphere of trust and camaraderie that rarely exists in civilian institutions. Doors in the barracks are not locked, providing a visible reminder of the trust that is part of the ethic required of leaders in combat as well as in peacetime. Violation of the Honor Code in any point may be grounds for an Honor Board and subsequent dismissal. An Honor Board is similar to a court of law in which the cadet is called to testify about his behavior and a judgment is made by a panel who determine whether the code has been violated and whether separation is necessary.

In order to continue study at USMA, a cadet is required to maintain a certain grade average, called a QPA (Quality Point Average). Falling below a minimum QPA places the cadet on academic probation, meaning that he or she is not guaranteed any leaves or passes without the written approval of the company TAC officer, who may also require the cadet to receive Additional Instruction or to attend extra required study periods. Weekend trips, even with airline tickets already purchased, might not be granted during academic probation, but this means that the cadet in question has the opportunity to focus more sharply on getting the grades back in shape. It is a balancing act to survive West Point, and emotional and physical struggles can interfere with academic performance there just as they can anywhere else; West Point simply has a lower tolerance than many schools for letting academic standing get out of balance. If a cadet's grades drop below the minimum QPA, the cadet's file is taken before an Academic Board for review and possible academic probation; if probation does not result in improved grades, a final review by the Academic Board can result in the cadet's separation. Unlike an Honor Board, an Academic Board does not allow the cadet to address or even attend the proceedings. All the academic department heads sit on the board, along with the Dean. Perhaps because of the difficulties of coordinating so many schedules, it can take some time for an Academic Board to convene and make a decision, creating a sort of limbo for cadets in peril of separation. During the Academic Year, they might be enrolled in the spring term when they receive word that their preceding term's standing has resulted in dismissal. When word of separation comes at the end of AY, a cadet in field training will be moved to transient barracks until out-processing is completed. It is actually possible for a cadet to be unsure of academic status up until graduation, if it is a borderline case; just as in other schools, if the minimum grade average is not maintained, a degree will not be granted. Of course, this also delays the commissioning of an officer, so, as in most of the challenges presented by USMA, it's complicated.

In general, if separation occurs during the first two years at West Point, things move along much like a college transfer, academically, and there is no resultant financial or military obligation. However, after the Commitment at the beginning of the third (Cow) year, a cadet is obligated to repay the Army for the education provided by USMA. Even if the time at USMA is cut short, a military service obligation (or in some cases a financial obligation) must still be fulfilled. That can mean serving as an enlisted, rather than commissioned, member of the Army. The exception to this is academic separation; even late in the 47-month adventure, academic separation does not obligate a cadet to repay tuition or serve immediately in the Army.

Re-admission may be a possibility following separation. If your cadet wants to pursue that, it will require going through the same process that led to the first appointment: nomination by a member of Congress, physical examination, fitness assessment, recommendation letters, academic application. The challenge, of course, will be to demonstrate to the admissions board that whatever problems led to the separation have now been overcome and will not happen again. That's tough, but cadets have been through tough places before—they train for tough situations all day, every day.

To return to the heart, though, because that's where moms tend to live, regardless of the specific procedures involved in separation, it will be a difficult experience for your cadet and for you. You're not likely to be taken completely by surprise if separation comes; it's a slow process and the deliberations take a while, so there's a bit of a waiting game involved regardless of the causes. Support your cadet by remaining positive and encouraging; by giving him or her time to reflect and process feelings before expressing them; and by remembering that the person who may be coming back to live at home is not the child who left home before R-Day, but a young adult who is quite capable of making decisions and moving forward from this place. Just the idea of making decisions about the future can be challenging for a cadet leaving the Academy; plans for work, graduate school, marriage, and pretty much everything else have been dependent on the needs of the Army ever since R-Day. The 47-month experience was to be followed by a 60-month period of service with most major choices being made by the Army. Having the freedom to choose again is simultaneously exciting and daunting. Ideally, you want to let your cadet know that your love and pride is not based on enrollment at USMA; that knowledge alone can provide a lot of strength and resiliency as decisions about the future are made and implemented.

In the end, there is really nothing moms can do to keep separation from happening, so don't spend time worrying about it. On the other hand, there are probably things we could do that might make it more likely, such as making our cadets' lives more stressful by talking about our own fears about separation. In every worthwhile endeavor, there is a possibility of failure. Don't let the aura around West Point separation cause you to be haunted by the specter of failure, and don't let the idea that your cadet could be asked to leave the Academy feel like a threat to you personally, as if the failure would be your own. Remember that you are not the one meeting or failing to meet USMA requirements, nor will you be the one directly living through the consequences of that success or failure. As ever, if your cadet is faced with the possibility of separation, your job is to be supportive and encouraging and proud.

Yes, be proud, even if separation is part of your West Point experience. A cadet who fails to meet one of the extremely high standards at West Point is still a remarkable young person with a great deal to offer to the world. Separation is just a forced redirection along the road to success.

CHAPTER 17
Authos
(being excused from required activities)

"Authos" (Authorizations) means getting out of things. Cadets like to get out of things! What kinds of things, you wonder? Parades, drills, and duties are the main activities cadets are permitted to miss once they gain authos. In literal terms, authos means a cadet is authorized to miss something that is generally required of others.

When a cadet has authos, it often includes the much-coveted ability to leave West Point and go somewhere else. It doesn't really matter where—anywhere will do! Those stony walls tend to make cadets feel closed in, trapped, and stir crazy. Since Plebe year restrictions are the strictest, after surviving Beast, the top priority for your Plebe might be gaining authos.

Corps squad athletes automatically have authos. They will be leaving post for competitions, games, practices, etc. Team practice interferes with drill practice, so athletes typically don't practice for the plethora of parades. Travel also means missing certain duties. Of course, all cadets must still meet standards of the Corps and athletes may have other duties assigned to make up for some missed.

For those who do not compete on a Corps squad team but still want to see new sights, it is necessary to figure out how to find the time to participate in an activity that leaves post. While all cadets can walk into Highland Falls on the weekends, they will quickly run out of things to do there. It's a quaint little village, but there's basically nothing to do, so it makes for a short trip. Sports competitions offer the chance to get further away than Highland Falls, and all cadets can compete in sports at the club level. These are not official Corps squad teams representing the Academy, but are instead categorized as competitive teams and sports under the DCA (Directorate of Cadet Activities). Included in these sports are water polo, rugby, handball, and boxing (to name a varied few). Cadets travel regionally for competitions so as to keep costs affordable, but some travel nationally, too. West Point has dozens and dozens of sports clubs available for cadets, and all of them are potential sources of authos. (If you are interested in seeing what is available through the DCA, you can see their website at www.usma.edu/uscc/dca. A gentle reminder, moms: this information is provided so you can see there actually is plenty to do... just in case your cadet says there is nothing. It's not provided for you to make suggestions, as that would cross the line into helicoptering, and we wouldn't want to do that, would we?)

Academic endeavors can also help your cadet get off post (and therefore out of duties). West Point offers clubs in any academic area your cadet can imagine. Many of these clubs relate to your cadet's chosen major, but some are just formed around subjects of interest. Cadets can even suggest new clubs and activities to be sponsored by the Academy. These clubs meet regularly on post and travel to activities that are off post. For example, the Arabic club might go to a cultural dinner in Connecticut, while the Model United Nations might travel to England for a competition.

Cadets can find clubs to join in areas of support (Scouting, band, choirs), hobbies (snowboarding, chess, bowling), and religious affiliation (both denominational support and outreach to others). No matter what your cadet is interested in doing, there is no need ever to be bored or feel stuck on post. With dozens of club activities to enjoy, your cadet just needs to get out there and join something.

Once Plebe year is over, as a Yuk your cadet can leave post every weekend with OPPs (Off-Post Privileges). Privileges increase with each passing year, but authos can still be earned to provide more opportunities for a change of pace. In seeking authos, your cadet will likely find new friends and perhaps try some new activities, even with the ulterior motive of getting out of something and away from West Point... for just a little while.

CHAPTER 18

The Time of His Life
(opportunities available through West Point)

While West Point offers some great opportunities, some cadets take advantage of this more than others. One particular cadet seemed to show up in every picture of "cool things" cadets get to do, so I asked his mom to write this chapter. Pretty much everything mentioned as an option here has been done by her son.

Many a homesick, dejected cadet has become even more homesick and more dejected after comparing notes with his friends who headed off to "normal" colleges. While he is suffering through Beast Barracks and Plebedom, his civilian counterpart is having "the time of his life." That's what they all think, anyway, and not entirely without reason.

While Plebes are sweating it out with uniforms and formations, the Chain of Command, SAMIs and WAMIs, and the extraordinarily demanding trio of academics, military instruction, and physical training, their civilian college friends are having one big party after another. College is famous for "all-nighters," but an all-nighter at West Point looks a lot different than an all-nighter at a regular school. How many civilian students stay up all Friday night scrubbing floors? Civilian college students also own their weekends; cadets do not.

But things aren't always what they seem.

After a cadet gets past Beast Barracks and adjusts to Plebedom, he will see that West Point offers a vast array of everyday college experiences, but, beyond the usual, opportunities abound for just about anything.

Possibilities for all sorts of foreign travel present themselves at every turn. And it isn't the run-of-the-mill travel of the everyday tourist. For one thing, it's free. Also, cadets see far more than visitors are generally allowed to see. As honored guests of the inviting government, cadets are given a backstage pass, so to speak, to the host country.

At home, cadets are given all manner of occasions to meet all manner of celebrities and dignitaries. They are regularly celebrated as guests on network television shows. Every four years they are invited to participate in the presidential inaugural parade. Science nerds get the once-in-a-lifetime chance to work with world-class scientists on developing the ultimate robotic hand or some other cutting-edge medical or technological device. Politically inclined cadets are granted internships in the United States Congress and access to the offices of policymakers, high-ranking generals, former presidents, and other notables. Cadets with an interest in national security may apply for top-secret clearances and be invited behind the scenes at the Central Intelligence Agency or Drug Enforcement Administration. The Glee Club routinely sings before the most distinguished of audiences— from the Super Bowl all the way to the Pope. The Model

United Nations team makes regular trips to places like Singapore and Taiwan, and if they happen to be in Oxford for Halloween time, there may be an invitation to a costume party in a real English castle.

On a more mundane level, cadets can get a national Emergency Medical Technician certification or sign up to help care for puppies who are being raised to be service dogs. Ike Hall offers world-class theatrical performances, from the ballet to plays to concerts, and every cadet has a season pass. Cadets who wish to be more than spectators can volunteer to take a turn as stage hands. And how often do civilian college students have Walker, Texas Ranger, as a guest in the cafeteria? West Point habitually plays host to throngs of heavy hitters in the fields of entertainment, publishing, journalism, and politics, to name a few, and there is no knowing who is going to show up to join the cadets for lunch.

When it comes to athletics, West Point has every sport imaginable. Not too many civilian colleges have parachute teams, and how many offer ice skating for a physical education elective? For fans of more winter fun, there are ski slopes right on post.

Not to be forgotten is the semester abroad, offering more adventurous cadets the chance to experience total immersion in the culture of their choice.

There is every reason why *The Princeton Review* once placed West Point in the Top Ten of all American colleges in the area of, among other things, "most to do on campus." No matter how bleak it may look at the outset, once a cadet figures things out and hits his stride (and things do improve considerably after Plebe year), the reality is that, compared to the garden-variety civilian college, West Point offers a far better shot at "the time of his life."

CHAPTER 19

Getting the Heck Out of Dodge
(leave and passes)

The cadets have a Facebook page they enjoy visiting called "My Life is Grey." This page is a cynical look at all things West Point. Imagine being stuck someplace where the buildings are gray, the uniforms are gray, the river is gray, and in winter the snow is gray. Winters are long in New York, and even in the other seasons the stress of USMA can have cadets feeling pretty gray. The cadets need to see other colors (perhaps to lose some of the cynicism?); they need and long for a break. Like the cornered desperadoes in an old Western television show, they'd like nothing more than to "get the heck out of Dodge." Cadets have two opportunities for a change of scenery (not including authos—see that chapter for more details): leave and pass.

Generally, all cadets are authorized leave as a part of the curriculum and as a break from academic and military duties. Unless otherwise notified, cadets may take leave from West Point during Thanksgiving, December holiday leave period, spring break, and some time during the summer. Of course, they might not come home during all of these breaks. Sorry, mom.

Cadets on West Point teams might have shortened leave periods due to training. (For example, my "poor" cadet missed some of Christmas leave every year as he was required to be in Puerto Rico with the dive team. The team stayed there well into Reorganization week, causing him to miss many tedious meetings. Sometimes, life is rough.) The parachute team also has a shortened Christmas leave due to their training in Arizona.

Some cadets choose to take trip sections (trips scheduled by a club, team or academic department) during breaks. As parents, we want our cadets to come home and visit; however, how can a college student turn down an opportunity to see the world and travel with friends, at little or no cost?

Sometimes a cadet might land on the proverbial "naughty list" and be denied leave. This can mean simply not getting permission for any number of reasons, but the permission may be denied because the cadet has to walk hours—which means walking back and forth in a courtyard between the barracks under the supervision of a senior member of Chain of Command. Some cadets have earned so many hours due to breaches of personal discipline that they will never be able to walk them all during the Academic Year. Those cadets might have a shortened leave so they can spend some extra time walking the Central Area. This punishment depends on the Commandant.

When the Corps has a general leave time, West Point will set up buses to and from the major New York City airports. The USMA website parents' page will list the times both for bus pick-up and drop-off and for ticket sales. Sometimes planes are late or weather causes delays, but not to worry. The cadets are trained in how to navigate New York City's public transportation, and they can get back to post—eventually.

A pass is different than leave. Everyone qualifies for leave, but not everyone qualifies for a pass. A pass is a privilege that may be earned but might not be granted. The pass can be requested as long as the cadet is not required for any scheduled duty or training. It is approved or disapproved by the company Tactical Officer (TAC). Plebes are eligible for one pass during each semester. Typically Yearlings receive two passes per semester, Cows receive three, and Firsties have unlimited passes. Opportunities exist for cadets to earn or take additional passes. Some cadets wishing to travel to an away sporting event may apply for a special pass called a spirit pass. Your cadet could earn an additional pass as a company reward for exemplary performance. Occasionally the entire Corps is rewarded with additional passes for a major accomplishment, like a big win on the football field.

Passes can be denied. Many a cadet (and cadet mom) has been disappointed when a pass was not granted. Just because the cadets may have an unused pass and a three-day weekend doesn't mean they'll get to enjoy it. A cadet who is in good academic standing and in good shape on the APFT should be positioned to obtain passes. However, passes can be disallowed for inappropriate behavior, disrespect, honor violations, and professional misconduct. A good rule of thumb is never to purchase airfare until the pass is in hand. However, some TACs will not approve passes until a day or two before the requested time. Many parents and cadets gamble in order to take advantage of fares on sale, but many are also left with an unusable ticket.

Sometimes West Point offers transportation to airports on major holiday pass weekends, but they do not always. Again, the cadets are trained and skilled at finding a way to get to the airports.

Unfortunately, from time to time life just happens and you need your cadet home for a family emergency. In this case, the TACs may approve emergency leave requests. If you are ever in this situation and cannot contact your cadet, you can contact the TAC directly. The contact information is available on the West Point home page.

As a West Point Mom your job will be to encourage your cadet to keep in great shape physically, militarily, and academically. They don't always appreciate this type of advice. However, the cadet who heeds it and keeps a "clean nose" will be positioned well to enjoy an extra break from the bleak winter gray of West Point.

CHAPTER 20

You've Got Mail!
(writing to your cadet)

O K, let's talk about writing. First of all, we realize that writing, actually composing thoughts on paper, is not something most people enjoy. However, while your beloved child is completely out of contact with you, not only during Beast Barracks, but also, to be perfectly frank, for a lot of the time at the Academy, you might find it comforting to do a little writing. It might even help you maintain your composure. It may also help your cadet maintain sanity. You know your son or daughter best, but my son says the letters are what got him through Beast.

If letters are so important, then what they say must be pretty critical. So, what should you write? Don't be daunted by the importance of the subject matter: anything from home will be fine. Talk about what the siblings are up to, the restaurant you tried last week, the construction going on in town, the progress of the garden, Dad's latest new account at work, the next home improvement project, the good-looking produce at the grocery store. Anything that is not Long, or Gray, or a Line is welcome during that first summer, when a

New Cadet's world becomes insular, isolated, and enclosed. In the outside world, you'll be thinking about your New Cadet, seeing things you'd talk about in person, so just write those thoughts down and stick them in an envelope.

After Beast, once New Cadets are officially cadets, there is still a feeling at West Point that the world begins and ends at Thayer Gate. It's easy for cadets to forget that there is life outside of physical training, inspection, military drill, studying, and training others to do the same. Sometimes it's tough to catch a cadet to share by phone, so write down what you'd say if you could talk. Putting it in an e-mail or text is good; depending on your personalities, though, paper and pen and envelope and stamp may be better. Re-read that last clause: it *may* be better to write on paper, but you know best. There is definitely something to be said, though, for holding something that a loved one recently held (a letter), and for having it to treasure, carry around, re-read and re-touch as often as desired. Think of it as a long-distance hug that is perpetually reusable. Especially during the first summer when talking with your New Cadet is limited, but throughout the 47-month adventure, writing can be a way to stay connected.

IMPORTANT NOTE: When you write to your son or daughter, especially during Beast, if you want to hear back by mail, enclose an extra piece of paper and a self-addressed, stamped envelope. HELPFUL NOTE: A time-saver, in both directions, is to print up a sheet of address labels for sending mail to your cadet. This way you always have the address correct and it only takes a second to get it on the envelope. The labels can be used for return address on the envelopes you enclose, too. Some moms (well, at least one) kept writing paper, envelopes, stamps and two sheets of address labels (home address and West Point address) with them at all times during Beast summer.

For more ideas about writing, there are form letters available on some of the online support groups, and probably from other sources, that are especially fun during Beast. Feel free to make your own, though. These are like the notes you passed in elementary school: "I like you. Do you like me? Check yes ___ or no ___." It sounds hokey to make them, but we promise it feels fabulous to get them back, with your cadet's handwriting alongside your own, a conversation preserved on paper. You can ask exactly what you want to know, and you can include humor quite easily, tailored to your own special relationship with your son or daughter. With my son's permission, I've reproduced one from his first summer at USMA. He simply circled his responses and filled in some blanks, and we got a letter! It's included at the end of this chapter.

For younger siblings who want to stay in touch, writing letters may be a challenge. Have them try playing games through the mail, like slow-mo tic-tac-toe—make the board, place the first mark, and mail it to the New Cadet with a stamped, self-addressed, return envelope. The game is made more fun by writing challenges on the page, too, so there's the back-and-forth banter that would go on if they were playing face-to-face. There are other pencil and paper games that can be played this way, such as hangman or pen the pig. Drawing pictures for each other, no matter the level of artistic ability, is another approved Beast activity.

OK. Enough fun. What about serious matters like sending "howlers" during Beast? Howlers are envelopes that scream "LOOK AT ME" when they come through the mail. The term "howlers" gained notoriety as the means of communicating "you're in trouble" in the *Harry Potter* books. Bright colors (especially pink), stickers, fragrance, larger than standard size—all of these make a letter stand out when it comes in at mail call. There was a lot of talk about these one summer recently, and our opinion is that they are a bad idea. One upperclassman cadet, when asked his opinion of howlers being sent by parents "in fun," asked, "Do they just hate their kid or what?" For the most part, a New Cadet does not want to be noticed: the less attention, the better. Cadre will do their part to make each and every New Cadet feel exposed and uncomfortable as often as necessary; moms truly do not need to pile onto that and add insult to injury. It goes back to the idea that your young person is no longer your little child, but a competent adult in a professional training program at the highest level, making the first moves toward being a world leader. You have the choice of paying due honor to that role or of making light of it. Again, you know yourself and your cadet and your relationship; only you can make the final decision on this issue. Do consider the message you're sending not only to your cadet, but to his team members and his superiors, all of whom play critical roles in his success at USMA, where he has chosen (and has been selected) to begin his adult career.

There are restrictions during Beast, and there will be restrictions for all the phases of your cadet's military career, even after leaving the Academy. No packages, no candy, no food, no alcohol—the rules will depend on the environment. You've enforced rules for all the years you've been a parent; you've taught your progeny to follow rules and respect authority. Don't toss that out the window now. Keep leading by example: follow the rules for mail during Beast. They aren't official regulations, but they represent long tradition wisely recommended by those who've been through as New Cadets and as Cadre. The best envelope during Beast is the simplest—plain white, without adornments.

Why do things have to be so rigid during that first horrible summer? First of all, don't think of it as a horrible summer. It's hard, for your cadet and for you and for those who care about both of you. But, hey, childbirth—or adoption—was hard, and look what you got for it! Keep it in perspective. These are some of the most determined and capable young people in the nation, and they've enrolled in the premier leadership training program on the planet, and the system works. Trust it. In order to build leaders, the Academy program first must separate the trainees from other support so that they themselves learn to rely on the system, on Chain of Command, and on their team members. This is critical in business and educational leadership, if you think about it, but in a military environment such trust has life-and-death implications. The hard truth is that your cadet is very likely going to be in a war zone one day in the not-so-distant future, and success and survival there will depend on being part of a team that is trained and competent, relying on one another and a system that works. During the first summer that system has some pretty strange-sounding requirements and restrictions, but they're all necessary for the whole system to work.

Now, here's a tougher question, one that gets to the personal level, to a mom's heart: "Why doesn't my cadet write back?" First of all, it's our hope that if you take the advice from the beginning of this section about writing, it will be easier for your cadet to write back and you won't be asking this question. But if you haven't been able to implement our suggestions, or if you have but your cadet still doesn't write, here are a few things to know.

The United States Postal Service does deliver mail to the United States Military Academy, but that does NOT mean that it has been delivered to your cadet, particularly (unfortunately) during Beast summer. The mail arrives at the garrison post office (for the military post at West Point), then goes to the Academy post office, then gets put in cadets' boxes. That's all well and good. But in order to go to the post office during Beast, a New Cadet must get permission and must be escorted by a member of Cadre. This must happen during the limited summer hours of operation for the USMA post office, and those hours tend to be the same hours that Cadre has your cadet on the ground doing push-ups or running up and down hills or sitting in classes on etiquette or cleaning rifles. So, even though it may only take two days for your check to get to the Thayer Hotel to pay for reservations for your next visit to the Point, it may take a week or more for your precious missive to your New Cadet to arrive in the eager hands of its intended recipient. Toward the end of Beast, during the training in the field out at Camp Buckner, New Cadets are so busy that they may not even receive any mail until after March Back.

Second, see above paragraph. Your cadet spends hours every day doing things at someone else's bidding, following orders, working until he could probably fall asleep standing up in a chow line (and may have). He may carry your letter around in his pack for a few days, forgetting and remembering it, not having time to sit and read it. He may just want to kick back when he gets a moment "of his own." You wouldn't begrudge him that at home. You'd let him veg in his room or in front of the TV for a little while after a big exam, right? Figure this is exam time on steroids, for weeks on end. He needs major down time, and he's lucky if he gets any at all—even in the shower he might not be alone, due to time and facility constraints. Seriously. So cut him some slack, and remind your heart that he really does love you, despite the dearth of declarations of that love. Instead of grieving because he hasn't written, write again!

Sample Form Letter

Dear (Mom, Dad, Family, girlfriend, high school principal),

This is just a quick note to let you know I'm (well, happy, hospitalized, OK). So far, CBT has been (as expected, better than expected, harder than expected, easier than expected, unexpected). I've (lost, gained) weight, mostly because I (eat like an Army, like Army food, hate Army food, need more Army food) and I (never stop working, never stop eating, never stop sleeping, never stop).

I have a (decent, smelly, female, cool, difficult) roommate. He is _____ from _____. He plays (basketball, football, baseball, tennis, Pokemon). We enjoy (cleaning, studying, PT, storytelling, nothing) together.

So far, I've probably met (1, 10, 100, 1000, _____) New Cadets, and (10%, 50%, 80%, 99 44/100%) of them are (nice, jerks, smart, attractive, heavy perspirers). One guy reminds me of (several high school friends' names here, along with a Marine colonel and a Navy nurse he knew) because of his (skin tone, sense of humor, haircut, ball-handling, mustache, determination, friendliness). I think (younger brother) would like _____ because he's a (cut-up, kayak paddler, dancer).

The fireworks Saturday were (awesome, disappointing, as good as the ones near home, sad without you here). I (enjoyed, appreciated, missed, slept through) the concert. That West Point band really is (showy, talented, versatile, in uniform).

So far I have (shot live ammo, climbed a wall, made a bed, rappelled down a mountain, cleaned a toilet). I'm looking forward to (throwing a grenade, serving at dinner, sleeping tonight, seeing you).

After A-Day, I'd love to have (fudge, oatmeal raisin cookies, goldfish crackers, a real goldfish, my physics textbook).

That's it for now. Please keep (praying for, writing to, singing about) me.

(Yours truly,
Respectfully submitted,
Your most humble and obedient servant,
Cordially,
Love,)

_____

CHAPTER 21
Boodle
(sending care packages)

Boo • dle, noun. A large quantity of something.

Cadets love boodle! Boodle at West Point means anything yummy or entertaining, generally in a care package from home. After Beast, a cadet may keep as much boodle as will fit in a boodle box, a large, sealable plastic container that is roughly 23" x 17" x 9". Exact size varies as the box must fit on a certain closet shelf, and those sizes vary by barrack. The Post Exchange (PX), a department store on post for military personnel, stocks boodle boxes in the correct sizes for each of the barracks. By purchasing at the PX, your cadet can secure the largest possible storage container to keep all that treasured boodle. Purchasing the boodle box has become something of a tradition during A-Day weekend. This chapter contains input from several West Point Moms and is intended to help you come up with fun and creative ways of your own to fill your cadet's box.

On my son's Plebe year birthday, I mailed his birthday box to his coach. I wanted it to be a surprise. I had a cake delivered to team practice from a local company (www.loveacadet.com), and the rest of the "party" was in the box. Inside the box were tablecloth, party hats, goody bags (candy, bubbles, noise makers, etc.), and other treats. It was a nice surprise for my son's first birthday away from home.

One mom made her cadet 21 different kinds of cookies for his twenty-first birthday. It was a memorable box and he had plenty to share with classmates. But birthdays are just one opportunity for moms to get creative with boodle.

TEEs (Term End Examinations), also known as finals, bring another reason for boodle (as if there needs to be a reason). This is when I sent my cadet's very favorite goodies. I sent my first ever batch of Oreo Balls in his first ever TEE box. I even got a phone call: "OMG!! What are these white things?!" Now they're a boodle staple in cold weather months. (You'll find the recipe at the end of this chapter.)

I like to send things from home, too. One box included a bag of dog hair with a note: "Sprinkle on everything to feel right at home." He passed on that. A friend's mom took photos of the family pets, the garden flowers and random shots around the house and created a photo album using her state's license plate cut in half as the cover. It was a great spirit-lifter with reminders of home, and was small enough to store.

During the swine flu epidemic, I sent an "anti-swine flu" box. It included all kinds of vitamins, cold meds, chicken soup, hand sanitizer, tissue, face masks, pig gummies and a pig Pez dispenser. I decorated the box with pink piggies. The box was a huge success: he loved it and he didn't get swine flu.

Coupled with an electric hot pot, a hot chocolate package makes a nice cold weather box. With assorted flavors of hot chocolate mixes, chocolate covered marshmallows, and peppermint stick stirrers, a cold winter night is easier to bear, especially for those cadets from the warmer parts of the country. This box also contained some ceramic "cow" mugs, as it was sent during the cadet's Cow year.

If you are from a state with an active Parents' Club, your cadet is likely receiving boodle from them once or twice a year. Even if you are not a member, your cadet will get goodies. If you are not part of the packing or donating for whatever reason, you can always send a check to your club for supplies or to defray shipping costs. If you are on the team to prepare club boxes, be aware that local merchants and national companies have been known to help supplement the Parents' Club boodle shipments. States with unique commodities (such as Georgia peanuts) will donate to help fill the boxes. All you have to do is ask.

Sometimes boodle doesn't come in a box. One of my friends mailed a big red bouncy ball to her cadet. She just wrote the address on it in permanent marker, affixed postage, and mailed it. What a smile that must've brought to her cadet's face on a bleak West Point winter's day. Never mind the laughter of his friends when they saw it! I know of a mother who sent an empty hot pink laundry basket the same way. It was in response to a family joke, and the cadet still has the basket. If you're going to get this creative, it helps to be friends with your local post office staff. They never know what's coming through the door when they see you drive up.

A soda bottle can be easily turned into a shipping container. Fill with goodies after cutting off the bottom. When you're sure you're done, duct tape the bottom back on, label and ship. The mail clerk might look at you funny, but you really can mail the bottle as-is.

Don't forget Halloween or Easter with all the special dollar store fun to be explored. In October, send costumes and make up supplies and bags of candy, as the cadets trick-or-treat and come to dinner in costume. The Easter Bunny is a welcome visitor, and those little plastic eggs can be filled with all sorts of goodies. One mother sent fresh coconuts decorated as eggs to a cadet's classmate, who comes from American Samoa—a little touch of home!

The Gloom Period is the cold, dark January-through-March timeframe at West Point. Spirits can be as gray as the skies and the river and the walls. The Gloom calls for special boodle: marshmallow or Nerf guns, Nano bugs, kazoos, balloons, the absolute most favorite thing they like to eat, or a good movie on DVD and some microwave popcorn to go with it. Don't forget the Fizzies and the beef jerky. A mom sent her son his favorite snack—spicy hot boiled peanuts—and had to be creative about sending the glass jars. She wrapped each jar in newspaper and plastic bags and filled the entire box with spray foam insulation. The jars arrived intact, but it took the cadet two hours to cut them out of the hardened foam.

You can be creative with packing material that is a bit easier to unpack. Use rolled up comics from the Sunday paper or rolled up favorite magazines to surround more fragile items. Marshmallows (including circus peanuts) are good shock aborbers. One mom popped popcorn, packed it into sandwich-size zip-top bags, seasoned each bag with a different flavoring, and used the sealed, filled bags as packing cushions.

For those who do not want to bother with shipping, the

West Point area has boodle companies that are willing to deliver boodle to your cadet. Links for those companies are located in the parents' section of the USMA web page and are listed in a document on www.facebook/WestPointMoms.

Don't be shy about enlisting the help of other moms when you have an "urgent" boodle need. A mom who lives close to the Academy has, on more than one occasion, delivered a pot of homemade chicken soup to a sick cadet. Another mom, who upon learning her son's pass was not approved at the last minute, found a mom who happened to be going to West Point for the weekend. The traveling mom offered to buy all the favorite goodies the first mom had been stockpiling at home. While he didn't get a hug from his own mom, the cadet did get a box full of love and a big hug from a surrogate.

Nothing says love like a full cadet boodle box. Be creative and have fun packing it. Who knows? You might even get a phone call! You might also acquire a couple more cadets who call you "Mom" in anticipation of those fabulous boxes. One mom sent every box with a smaller package marked "for the kid across the hall." Don't be afraid to add an extra cadet to your Boodle list. It's all for the Corps—and they'll love you for it!

(For a special treat for your cadet, see the famous Oreo Ball recipe on the following page.)

Oreo Ball Recipe

Ingredients:

1 pkg. Oreos
1 pkg. cream cheese
White or dark chocolate bark

Soften cream cheese at room temperature. Pulverize Oreos (I use the food processor). Put all crumbs back in food processor with softened block of cream cheese and process until it's a ball. Refrigerate a few minutes, and then roll into one-inch balls. Place on wax paper. Place in freezer about 10 minutes. Melt chocolate according to package directions. Dip balls into chocolate and place on wax paper until chocolate hardens. You can drizzle white or dark chocolate on top for decoration.

CHAPTER 22
Whiter Whites? Not So Much
(cadet laundry)

I remember years ago having a friend at an elite college. She had maid service and laundry service. I thought that was a pretty great setup! While our cadets don't have maids, they do have the opportunity to send out their laundry. Many moms wonder how this whole laundry deal works, so we're throwing in a brief chapter to explain it.

Cadets are trained in how to deal with their laundry during Beast. That doesn't mean they all do it right, or that there are no errors, but the information is explained. The short story for basic laundry is that each cadet sorts it into mesh bags with an identifying tag attached. Cadets are to inventory what is in each bag. Theoretically, the clothes come back in the same bags they were sent off in, as the whole bag goes into the washer unopened. Realistically, however, that may not be the case.

Whether due to cadet error or laundry error, the laundry service is notorious for losing clothing or sending back items that do not belong to the cadet who sent them. I remember my son being rather upset Plebe year when his last khaki T-shirt disappeared. He wore a size small, and the laundry returned an extra-large. It was certainly frustrating, but somehow he survived. Perhaps it's all part of the West Point training: teaching the cadets to weather life's little inconveniences and figure out on their own how to make them right.

Due to allergies, all the machine washable clothes are washed in very hot water with no detergent. Therefore, like the walls and the weather, the whites are soon gray. Uniform pieces are sent to a separate area of the laundry, where they are cleaned and returned on hangers. Cadets keep an iron in each barracks room for touchups.

You might notice when you visit your cadet that shirts aren't as clean as you would expect. The cadets seem to wait as long as possible before sending their clothing to be cleaned. The daily uniforms can be washed in a machine, and if a cadet gets in a pinch and doesn't have time to wait for the laundry, coin operated washers and dryers are available in MacArthur and Grant barracks.

When the cadets find they have a wardrobe malfunction, such as a missing button or a broken zipper, or if they need patches sewn on or other alterations done, they can take the items to a place called WB-4. There they will find seamstresses and tailors who are very accommodating.

Cadets will find a way to get clean clothes. Some wait for mom to come visit. Others develop a good relationship with their sponsors and ask to use the washer and dryer during a visit. The truly ingenious (typically upperclassmen) find a way to get their dirty laundry to Highland Falls, where the nice people who run a laundry service will wash, dry, and fold it for them at a decent price per pound. No matter the method, our cadets at least have the option of looking spiffy and feeling fresh as a daisy!

CHAPTER 23

No Atheists in Foxholes
(opportunities for religious expression)

It is said of the regular Army "there are no atheists in foxholes." While this may or may not be so, at West Point, during Beast Barracks, it looks to be true on Wednesday nights. Each Wednesday evening during Beast is Chaplain's Time, where cadets have a time of worship and prayer, with fellowship and goodies provided by West Point families. For some cadets, food is the major draw. But for some, the break from the Cadre and the chance to relax and visit with fellow New Cadets is what brings them out en masse.

Each major religion has its own Chaplain's Time. The cadets learn pretty quickly which group has the best food. Don't be surprised if your Catholic son tells you he went to Latter-day Saints Chaplain's Time, as they are known for serving pizza. The New Cadets will often stick with their squad mates and try out a new religious group each week. If this happens and your cadet tells you about it, just relax. He is not turning his back on his upbringing; he's searching for air conditioning and food and people who smile at him instead of "speaking in a loud, authoritative voice."

At some Chaplain's Time meetings, a volunteer is manned with a camera. Cadets can sign up to have their pictures taken and e-mailed to moms. I have to admit, opening my inbox to see that smiling mug—while I was in the midst of missing him badly—absolutely made my day. You can also go to the West Point Parents' Facebook page (www.facebook.com/ WestPointParents) to see Chaplain's Time photos.

After the cadets survive Beast and the Academic Year begins, those interested in affiliating with a religious group will find many opportunities. Plebes may attend Club Night in the fall to learn of the choices available. At West Point, as on most college campuses, many faiths offer a group of some kind. Unlike most other campuses, however, West Point has a chaplain who is dedicated to promoting and educating the various religious communities on post.

As moms, we hope our kids will continue in the family religious traditions while at college. West Point makes this possible by offering services for the Protestant, Jewish, Latter-day Saints, Catholic, Muslim, and Buddhist faiths. However, with the killer schedule our cadets follow, do not be surprised to hear that weekends are used by your cadet to catch up on sleep rather than to seek out spiritual expression. The cadets will receive information on how/when/where to get involved in the faith of their choice, but since inquiring moms want to know these things, here are just a few of the many opportunities.

For the Catholic faith, there is a post chapel (Most Holy Trinity Catholic Chapel). In addition to Mass and Confession, the chapel offers religious education classes, cadet choir, United Catholic Fellowship (on Club Night), and many other opportunities. Cadets can learn about these from the Catholic Chaplain.

The Cadet Chapel is home to a collective Protestant Sunday worship time. Protestant services are also available at the Post Chapel and the Old Cadet Chapel. Cadets can join the cadet choir or the hand bell choir, teach Sunday school, or participate in one of a number of Bible study/fellowship groups on post. The largest Protestant group is Officer's Christian Fellowship. A few other Club Night groups include Baptist Student Union, Navigators, Canterbury Club and Chi Alpha. The Fellowship of Christian Athletes meets on Thursday mornings during breakfast. I Am Second meets on Thursday evenings and some Sunday mornings; its members schedule an annual missionary trip during Thanksgiving week.

The Jewish Chapel offers weekly Shabbat services, holiday celebrations, religious education classes, retreats, social gatherings, and other programs. Cadets can participate in the Jewish Cadet Squad and the Jewish Chapel Cadet Choir.

The Church of Jesus Christ of Latter-day Saints offers Sunday services on post. Institute is held on Tuesday nights during Club Time.

Islamic services and activities are held in the Cadet Interfaith Center. Trip sections and special services are a part of their offerings.

For the faith groups that are small in number, like Hindu, there are no formal services available on campus, but the chaplains extend support to affirm the faith choice of these cadets while providing for their private worship needs.

As you can see, the opportunities for religious education and ministry abound at West Point. Parents interested in learning more on R-Day can attend a New Cadet Parent

Worship Service and Luncheon at either Most Holy Trinity or the Cadet Chapel. If you or your cadet can't find what you are looking for, check with the post Chaplain's office. The Army chaplains are there to support your cadet spiritually during the 47-month adventure.

CHAPTER 24
Funny Money
(cadet accounts)

As parents, some of us really struggle with the way money works for cadets at West Point. It's an unusual situation, since cadets are still college students (read: children), but they are employed full-time and paid by the Army (read: adults). I had a very hard time just backing off and letting an 18-year-old deal with all his finances. However, he, like most cadets I've heard about, rose to the occasion. Just because inquiring parents want to know, here is some brief information on how the whole West Point money thing works.

Anything that is for personal use or consumption is paid for with "real money" (cash, debit card, credit card) belonging to and controlled by the cadet. Anything required by the Academy for school (books, cadet uniforms, some military issue items) comes out of cadet accounts, which are set up and maintained by the USMA treasurer. Because these latter transactions take place without any apparent "real money" changing hands, many cadets refer to the cadet accounts as "funny money."

Cadets are paid as E1's, the lowest ranking Army enlisted

persons, for four years. The bulk of this pay is deposited into their cadet accounts, but cadets receive an "allowance" each month from their pay. The amount the cadets actually see (and therefore control) ranges from approximately $225 monthly for Plebes to $500 monthly for Firsties. The first year, cadet accounts don't have enough money built up when the first bills need to be paid, so West Point asks for an initial deposit to open the account (in the $2000 range most years). The treasurer pays all the cadet's Academy-related bills from the cadet account, including laundry, haircuts, class fees, books, computers/technology, class ring, graduation expenses, etc.

In the cadet account, a cadet must keep what is called a "minimum account balance" (MAB). After Plebe year, a cadet may withdraw the difference between the account balance and the MAB. This is called "top off." Money withdrawn as top off goes to a bank account of the cadet's choosing (the one set up prior to R-Day). At this point, the "funny money" has transformed into real money. Some cadets leave the top off alone and have a nice little nest egg upon graduation. Other cadets use it for funding travel home or for spring break trips or for any number of other things—it's their money.

While it's natural for us moms to want to help out and tell our cadets how/what/why/when to deal with their money, it's just one more area where we must back away and allow them figure out things for themselves. Whether we are ready to believe it or not, our cadets really can handle this money thing.

CHAPTER 25
Ouchies and Boo-Boos
(managing mild illness)

Like most West Point Moms, I find out my son is sick or injured by cryptic Facebook posts—on his wall, not mine. My favorite: "Board wins!" (after a particularly bad contact with a diving board). Of course, since he is 845 miles away, there was not much I could do other than say, "Poor baby!" However, there are more helpful resources available at West Point.

Any time a cadet is sick or injured, if medical attention is desired, the cadet must report to "sick call" at the cadet clinic. Cadets are taught sick call procedures during Beast. The cadet clinic is inside the cadet area. They treat minor ailments and refer major ones to the post hospital (Keller Army Community Hospital).

While West Point doesn't encourage cadets to self-medicate, my cadet has found it easier to have a "sick box" for conditions we would normally treat at home. In the box he has ibuprofen, muscle cream, band-aids, cold and allergy medicine, cough drops and a thermometer. He also has emergency chicken soup that can be heated in the company microwave. At his age, he knows what he needs and often gets himself feeling better without a clinic visit. If cadets are so sick that they need to miss class, they know they must go to the clinic.

If a potentially serious or very painful condition develops during the evening or night, and self-help hasn't helped, a cadet may still get medical aid even though the cadet clinic is not open. If, after consulting Chain of Command, your cadet feels the need to be seen in the hospital, with Chain's permission transport may be arranged to get the cadet to Keller. The Central Guard Room (CGR) in the barracks area is manned 24/7, and there is an assigned duty driver there who will transport cadets to the hospital—that is part of the reason the driver is there. Cadets are all given this information, but they put it in the "I don't need this right now; dump it" part of their minds, and give it no thought until they do need it, at which time they may have forgotten. If you know it, too, you'll be able to remind your cadet if you get an urgent call in the middle of the night.

Serious conditions at any time of day, whether illness or injury, will win your cadet a trip to Keller. The medical staff there is top-notch. Injuries requiring surgery are treated there; there are physicians on staff who specialize in some of the more common injuries. Parents wishing to be on post during surgery often find accommodation at the 5 Star Inn (http://www.westpointmwr.com/ACTIVITY/5STAR), which has a location on post very close to Keller. If you want to stay there, unless you personally have military or Department of Defense credentials, a copy of your cadet's ID card must be on file with the 5 Star before a reservation can be made. It is simple to do this, and it can be done at any time;

IDs are kept on file by class year just in case they are needed. Your cadet can call the 5 Star (845-938-6816), speak to the person on duty and get an e-mail address for that person, then scan the front of the ID and e-mail it to that person.

Occasionally severe emergencies happen to cadets. If Keller is not equipped for the level of care your cadet needs, care will be provided at one of the excellent medical facilities in the surrounding area.

Having a sick or injured kid away from home is tough on a moms. Please know that West Point is going to take care of your cadet. Sick cadets may not receive the same TLC moms provide, but they definitely get the "C."

CHAPTER 26

More than a Boo-Boo
(when cadets need more than sick call)

I thought this book should include an example of how a serious injury is handled at West Point. I am grateful that I have no experience with this, so this chapter is from a contributing mom. Here's to hoping this is one chapter you never need to use for reference.

When someone tears an anterior cruciate ligament, he typically hears a popping sound. In case you don't know, you don't ever want to hear a popping sound in your leg. Especially if you've heard it in the same leg before. Five years earlier. And you're a Firstie at West Point.

Nonetheless, that's exactly what happened to our cadet on the last day of his CTLT training at Fort Bliss, Texas. All the adventures my son had planned for his final year at West Point seemed to come to a screeching halt. Not only did our Firstie lament the long recovery time from a painful surgery, but he also faced looming uncertainties about branching and graduation.

Clearly, surgery is not on your cadet's must-do list, but if surgery becomes necessary it might be useful to know a few things in advance. Individual experiences will vary, but here are a few things we learned along the way.

- First of all, when I contacted other West Point parents, I received helpful advice on how to assist my son. Thanks to repeated recommendations, I ordered some high-quality, performance crutches from MobiLegs (www.mobilegs.com). Imagine my delight when my cadet's fancy new crutches arrived the day before his surgery, and he had a glint of excitement about being able to use them for the next six weeks!

- Support the wishes of your cadet. If your cadet wants you to be there for the surgery, try to do it.

- Medical privacy and access to records will depend on your cadet. Once they are 18, of course, they must give permission for you to be included in medical communication. *(Author's Note: That's not an Army regulation; it's a Federal one.)* Be willing to abide by your cadet's personal decision in that regard.

- By hospital policy, your cadet is the only one who can ask for pain medication, but remember your cadet is obviously not the only patient. Even though your cadet may always be your baby, in the eyes of the Army and West Point your cadet is considered a competent adult and will be treated as such. More than likely your cadet will share a room with another military person, and not necessarily a West Point cadet, during the hospital stay. The rooms are small and lack privacy, so don't expect to be enjoying much space.

- If allowed, bring your cadet something good to eat,

just as you would in a civilian hospital. Our cadet definitely preferred the food from off-post, and that's a major understatement. Depending on the other person sharing a room with your cadet, if possible, extend an offer of food, magazines or any other items to make a hospital stay more pleasant.

• Hospital hours are enforced; respect them.

• After major surgery, don't be surprised if your cadet doesn't want to return immediately to the barracks. Your cadet might want to send up an exemption to policy memo to the TAC officer to go off post to recover for a couple of days.

• Roommates can be either a great help for your cadet or an impediment to rest and recovery. Encourage your cadet to be honest with roommates and friends so they can help.

When it was over, it was hard to say good-bye. I dropped my Firstie off at Grant turn-around, and then watched him crutch his way back to the barracks. In the end, to our delight, our cadet actually did better with this second ACL surgery than he did with his first one!

CHAPTER 27
The Other Woman
(getting along with girlfriends)

It's not news to any mom that a child's dating life has an impact on the family dynamic. Whether your cadet is a son or a daughter, if there is a girlfriend or boyfriend involved, West Point gets that much more complicated. For whatever reason, we tend to hear more about drama between moms and girlfriends than between moms and boyfriends. As a story about a relationship that worked, I hope this chapter will be helpful for moms of both male and female cadets.

My son had been gone for what seemed like years. I'd received a few letters and sent a few more. The week had arrived for the First Phone Call. My husband and I kept our cell phones closer than ever, and we stayed in. He'd probably call home, we thought, rather than calling one of us, because we had extensions at home and more of us could get on the line to hear his voice.

The first possible call day passed, a Sunday. He didn't call, but we knew to expect this. The directive was that during this week the New Cadets would be given opportunity to call home as duties and Chain of Command allowed. By this time we were beginning to realize that the activities we consider normal and simple in the "real" world were neither normal nor simple in the world of Cadet Basic Training. Just going to the post office required an escort, and that required a member of Cadre with free time, and that just didn't happen often during Beast. Thus, we weren't really surprised not to receive the First Phone Call on the first possible day. We were just eager to talk to the boy.

The next day we stayed near the phone again but did not receive the First Phone Call. Every time the phone rang we wondered; this was before we had put caller ID on our home phone, so we actually had to answer the call to find out who was on the other end. We knew from the R-Day briefing that this was the week, and that the phone calls happened a few at a time, and that different Beast companies had different schedules. We comforted ourselves with logic as the tiny dramas of thrill and hope and, alas, disappointment, played out several times, and we went to bed another night without knowing when we would talk to our son.

Tuesday. No First Phone Call. By the afternoon, my husband was getting a little stir crazy, and for some unknown reason he thought I could use a bit of a diversion. I really can't imagine what made him think I needed a break. Regardless, he suggested, and I agreed, that we could take the younger siblings, who really could use a break from the mini-dramas, and go out to dinner. We would both take our cell phones and make sure they worked wherever we ended up. Our New Cadet would call the cell phones, probably mine, if he got no answer at home, we reasoned.

Just as we walked out of the restaurant after dinner, my cell phone rang. I grabbed it (or maybe I'd been holding it in one hand all through dinner, okay?) and answered the call from... the girlfriend.

I answered cheerily, "Hi! We haven't heard anything yet, sorry."

"He just called me."

My heart leaped again. "Oh, well, I'd better hang up. I hope he'll know to call my cell phone, because we're out to dinner."

She broke down in tears. "I'm sooo sorry."

This was unexpected. Was something wrong with our son? "Sweetie, what is it?"

"I told him to hang up and call you first. I told him he shouldn't have called me. I told him to hang up. I'm so sorry."

"But?"

"But he told me he couldn't." She was choking out the words. "He said if he hung up he wouldn't be able to make another call, and we just had a few minutes, and so I had to let him talk." More sniffles. "I am sooo sorry."

Even now, years later, looking back, I choke up as I remember the conversation. How it blessed me to have a young woman so committed to my son, and to his family, that she would have given up her own time with him in deference to me. How glad I was that his heart was lifted by spending a few moments talking with her. It never occurred to me to be angry that he had called her. I was not angry with him nor angry with her. My son, the boy who left home to join the Corps of Cadets, was a man now, and he needed a woman, and a beautiful, talented, strong, devoted woman was there for him when he called. Yes, he could have talked to his beautiful, talented, strong, devoted mother, but this young man did not need a mom. He needed a soul-mate, a companion, someone to walk alongside him and share the adventure, someone to admire and encourage and inspire him in a way I could not. Oh, how grateful I was in that moment that he had such a friend! I laughed as she explained, and as she shared the details of their visit—laughed with joy to know he was all right, and with gladness to realize he had received at least a few moments' pleasure, and with amusement that we'd been so careful with our phones and hadn't needed them after all.

A few days later I saw some friends with sons the same age as mine, sons who had gone to college nearby and were still living at home. I told my friends that my son had called— his girlfriend.

"He what?!"

Their shocked response startled me, but the wisdom of the West Point Mom had already begun to develop. I realized all at once that yes, my son was a man now, and these dear friends who knew so much about me and about him really could not understand that. I saw clearly that my son's choice to follow his dream had changed him and me, and had set us apart from our peers in ways we probably would not have predicted even if we had tried to guess our futures. So I said to my dear friends, from my position on this side of the Gray Divide, that I had realized my son was not my little boy any more. He was not even my big boy. He was in the Army. He was a young man. And young men, I told my aghast friends, do not need their mothers in the way that big boys do. He needed a woman, though, and she was there for him, and I, his mother, who wanted above all for him to have what he needed—I was glad he had called his girlfriend.

I could have gone off on my son's girlfriend. I could have

taken it as a personal insult that she had talked to my son and that he had not called me. I could have imagined that he and she had some prior agreement that he would call her; I could have created a fiction that I came to believe as true, that she was conniving and sneaky and unworthy of my friendship or my son's attentions. Would that have drawn him any closer to me, or made me miss him any less? I think not.

If your son has a girlfriend, think about this: He's in the Army. He is in the United States Army. Yes, he's a college student, and he'd like to do some college student things, but people his own age are enlisted in the Army and fighting battles right this minute. He knows this and can understand it better than any ordinary college student because he's taking military training and studying military history and discussing military issues every day of his life. That's not all, though.

He's also dressing himself in clothes his mom did not wash, dry, press, fold, hang, or put in his drawer. He's eating meals his mom did not cook at a table his mom did not set. He's waking up miserable and making himself go on anyway without any calling, begging, wheedling, threatening, or cajoling from his mom. He's working so hard that it literally makes him throw up, and his mom is not cleaning up the mess. He's getting sick and figuring out how to care for himself, facing challenges and learning to reward himself, failing and succeeding every day without his mom's involvement. This is no boy we're talking about. This young man has chosen a young woman as his girlfriend.

My experience with "the girlfriend" has been, without exception, positive. The only challenges I have faced that involved her had to do with how many people we could fit into the minivan for a trip to West Point, because we have a large family and we choose to include her in our number. She's been the only girlfriend for my son since they were juniors in high school, and they committed to being part of the 2% Club at West Point—the few who make it all the way through the four years as a couple. Since I know not everyone's girlfriend experience has been so smooth, I'll share a bit of what we did in the hopes that it will make your journey smoother.

We invited her on all but one trip to West Point. She went to R-Day, A-Day, and PPW, and she went with me on other trips there as well. We helped each other dress and do hair for the banquets. The one trip she didn't go on was during an autumn weekend when she was going up on her own soon afterward, and my husband wanted the weekend to be focused more on the younger siblings. The rest of the time, though, I thought that since she was a main support for my son, and since they wanted that support to continue into the future, I could help him by bringing her to him. Most of their dating life was on iChat; if I could help them have some real face time, I considered it a gift to my son that I was more than willing to give. Financially, it was no cost to me; she bought her own meals on the trips and stayed with us wherever we stayed.

I picked her up and dropped her off at airports in New York when her college schedule didn't allow her to make the drive with our family. It's what I would do for a friend. We offer to do that sort of thing for other West Point Moms or their cadets because we're "family." Well, this young woman was likely going to be family (and she is indeed engaged to marry my son as I write this). The least I could do was pick her up at an airport to save her the trouble and time and expense of train and cab fare. She (or he) paid her plane fare; she worked during college and saved almost all her money for trips to see him.

She went with me to the airport almost every time my son flew home, the exceptions being the two times he flew home and surprised her. Plebe year, she picked him up and brought him to me as a surprise once, too. Sometimes she knew his schedule when I didn't. We called and checked in with each other to make a plan about meeting and going to the airport each time. We waited together for him to arrive, and we watched together as he left through security. We had a routine, an order for doing things, when the good-byes came. My son gave hugs and handshakes to younger siblings and dad, then to me, and last to his girlfriend. I respected that. It's time. He's a man. When he leaves U.S. soil to go to a foreign deployment, I hope he'll give his wife a good, long hug as the last thing he does before going. Again, as far as we know, this is going to be his wife.

As in the one weekend when she didn't go with us to West Point, there were a few times when we did not ask her over, or when we asked our son to be home without her. The younger siblings felt that the girlfriend relationship took priority when she was here, and they didn't want to intrude; they felt freer to hang out with big brother when his girlfriend was not here, until they got used to the new way of being a family with one member living nine hundred miles away. With just short weekend visits, the younger ones wanted a little time of their own. So we let our son know that one of the evenings home would be a family night, without his girlfriend. That helped smooth the transition, and because we were honest about the need to have him here and respectful of his need to be with his girlfriend as well, there was no feeling possessive or rejected in all this time sharing. We all behaved as adults, and while there were hard moments, we worked through them together.

My cadet is not my only son, and I don't know as surely who the others will chose as a mate. When we as moms aren't so sure that a girlfriend is the chosen one, the intended for a lifetime, can we still pay this respect to our son's adult choice? I think we can. I think we can treat a young lady as a worthy recipient of a son's attentions, since he has already deemed her to be so. I think we can take a long view, with the benefit of years, and know that if we treat this girlfriend as if she is going to become part of the family, we will be building a stronger base for a future marriage for that son. If she does not become a daughter-in-law, we still will have gained more trust from the young man we love. Also, if we treat his decision with respect, he will gain confidence in his ability to choose well, which just might inspire him to choose more wisely the next time. If he knows mom will treat a girlfriend well, and that he doesn't have to prove his independence by choosing someone mom won't like, he is more likely to bring in a girlfriend he truly treasures, and less likely to use a girlfriend as a way to irritate his mother.

With good manners and patience, then, we can get through these 47 months, even with another woman involved. By taking a long view—working toward a future and not just struggling through the present—we can survive bad girlfriends, enjoy good girlfriends, and develop stronger relationships with adult sons who make us proud in every way—even in their choices for female companionship.

CHAPTER 28

Missing and Missed
(adjusting to yet another part of Army life)

A lthough it is normal for the family to do some adjusting when a child goes to college, USMA offers more opportunities than most schools for families to learn to do things differently. Important family events provide the platforms for some of these learning experiences.

Funerals, weddings, graduations, mitzvahs, christenings, even birthdays still happen, even when the family is not all together. For our family, the first of these came during Beast: an uncle died. The death was not unexpected; the uncle had been fighting a losing battle with cancer since the previous year's end. When the news of his passing came, though, our New Cadet was just past the first phone call home, and as a mom I didn't know quite what to do. I'm glad, really, that we didn't have to tell him the news on the first call. We'd been praying for this uncle daily, for months, and I knew my son would want to know the news, so I composed the letter. I was a bit unsure how he would receive it, though, in the context of the stress of Beast, so I asked for help. I contacted the

Chaplain's office. Chaplains are trained to serve in situations just like this. They served our family well in our relatively minor crisis.

After I explained the situation, the Chaplain told me someone would go to contact our son in person within a day or two, depending on the demands of the training schedule, to see how he was doing. I gave my permission for the Chaplain to deliver the news to my son if the letter had not arrived. As it happened, the Chaplain did arrive before the letter, so he gave the news to our son and was able to provide personal support as needed. While we knew that being excused from Beast for a non-immediate relative's funeral was not an option, the Chaplain's office did have authority to bestow another gift. Completely unexpectedly, then, we received a call from our New Cadet! He had handled the news without a problem, but the Chaplain had offered him a phone call, and he had gladly accepted.

We learned through this experience that there is a support structure in place at USMA, as in all of the military, to help its members in times of family need. Whether a chaplain, a counselor, or a member of Chain of Command, someone will be there for your cadet if there's a difficult family event that must be missed. Your role, then, is to take care of yourself and those at home, and to remind yourself as often as necessary that your cadet will be fine.

On the other side of things, if the missed event is a happy one, there is a different kind of support ready for your cadet. For one thing, the schedule at West Point is so intensely busy that there is very little time to sit around missing home and family. Additionally, cadets are surrounded by others who have missed family events and lived through the experience;

the temporary disappointment of not being present will be replaced by a strengthened bond of shared "suffering" (or celebration) with comrades in the profession of arms. This is an important bond, one that will help your cadet in the future at West Point and beyond. Comfort yourself with that thought.

Comfort your cadet (and yourself) by calling or texting a bit more than usual, perhaps. If there's enough time before the event, send up a package of fun—food or games or anything that will either take the mind off what's being missed or offer a sense of connection to the event in absentia. Suggest an activity, if one comes to mind, that means getting out of the barracks and having fun. The facilities at West Point are phenomenal, and DCA has activities available all the time; additionally, there are numerous other diversions for every season within a few miles of campus. (See our chapter, "The Time of His Life," for more on this topic.) If you have a way to take and send pictures electronically, you can offer an immediate view of what's going on; of course you'll have to determine if that will hurt or help morale. Here's a radical idea: ask your cadet ahead of time if seeing pictures will hurt or help!

Missing events is bound to happen. When someone joins the Army, it's understood that some things at home will be missed. However, the same thing can be said about attending any college far from home, taking a semester abroad, or even getting a job right in the neighborhood. Adult responsibilities require adult decisions, and they're not always easy ones. West Point just gives us a chance to make more of those than most people do, so we get to learn more than most people do in a given four-year period.

See? It's good for you. You're growing up!

CHAPTER 29

A Home Away from Home
(sponsors)

During the summer of Beast, the halfway point is marked by an event called the Ice Cream Social, where Army families assigned to West Point open their homes to several cadets, and the cadets spend the afternoon eating "real" food (and ice cream), watching TV, catching up on social networks, calling parents and girlfriends/boyfriends, and sleeping. Cadets on Corps squad teams often go home with a coach or assistant coach. A few very brave cadets spend the day with the Superintendent at his residence, Quarters 100. Some cadets bond with their Ice Cream Social host family and want to continue the relationship, but most cadets will find their official West Point sponsors through a different process.

During Reorgy week, each Plebe will have the opportunity to apply for a sponsor, a member of the military who volunteers to help cadets adjust to life at West Point and learn more about life in the Army. Those interested in the sponsor program are sent a questionnaire to complete, describing themselves so that they may be matched to a suitable sponsor. Plebes can be as detailed as they choose on this. They may indicate which interests (hobbies, sports, regional origins, etc.) are of key importance to the match. The sponsors have filled out similar forms. After both groups submit the questionnaires, the Plebes are matched with their sponsors.

As with all social relationships, especially arranged ones, some people click and some don't. Typically, new sponsors invite their cadets to their homes to get acquainted. The success of the program depends on both the cadet and the sponsor being willing to reach out to one another. My son was fortunate to have a relationship that worked. His sponsor was from the Southeast; the sponsor's wife was as well, and she requested Southern cadets, so no one would make fun of her accent. This wonderful couple provided my son with SEC football and sweet tea. Through spending time with them, my son was able to see what a military family was like, since he is not from one. The relationship continued until my son's Cow year, when the sponsor's time at West Point came to an end.

Some cadets don't participate in the official sponsorship program, but do build relationships through other avenues such as getting to know professors, coaches, TACs, etc. Other cadets might accompany a friend to a sponsor's home.

As a mom, I liked knowing that my cadet had a place to go where he could feel both taken care of and a part of a family. I am grateful that he had such a caring sponsor. I would advise any mom to encourage her Plebe to try out the program. Where else are Southern cadets going to get sweet tea in New York?

CHAPTER 30
Adopt-a-Cadet
(taking care of cadets in tight places)

It is often said that the military is like a big extended family and that West Point is part of that family. The shared struggles surrounding military service create a bond that is unusual in its depth and strength. Delivering boodle to cadets who didn't grow up in our own homes is just one expression of that. There are other ways that West Point Moms take care of one another and one another's cadets, especially when those cadets find themselves in tight places or unexpected predicaments. Being a mom implies relationship, and at West Point we get to expand that relationship to include all those in uniform and their families as well. It's sort of like adopting a few hundred children, though you'll only get to know some of them, one at a time. The family way is to treat other cadets the way we'd like our cadets to be treated. In doing so we give and receive aid in times of crisis, discouragement, and loneliness.

Travel often gives rise to crisis or discouragement and therefore presents opportunities to treat one another as family. Cadets travel during the busiest times of the year, and that can mean long layovers, delays and missed flights.

Add to crowded airports and overbooked airlines the fact that winter weather in New York can wreak havoc on connections, as can the weather in connecting or destination airports, regardless of the season. West Point Moms have been known to drive through blinding snow to rescue stranded cadets and offer a place to stay during an unplanned layover. During a planned layover, a West Point Mom once delivered an entire homemade continental breakfast buffet to a group of cadets in transit.

There are other ways to help when cadets fly. One West Point grandmother offered to let a cadet park his vehicle at her home near the airport during an extended overseas visit. We offer rides to and from airports for cadets moving through, and it is not unusual to find someone offering to drive two or more hours one way to deliver an "adopted" cadet from the airport to an assignment on short notice or to get a cadet home after an airline re-routing.

When visiting West Point, most moms find it quite natural to include an extra cadet in meals or trips or activities. Giving cadets a lift to the train station across the river in Garrison, taking cadets on a shopping trip, or including cadets in a family day at the park or apple orchard are all standard operating procedure when visiting our own cadets.

West Point Moms who live near training facilities or military posts get extra opportunities to share care through this special relationship. They often offer to be in-town family for "adopted" cadets on assignment. This can take the form of rides for most any reason, home-cooked meals in a family setting, or simply directions to the nearest mall or Starbucks.

We keep a list on the West Point Moms Facebook site—for those who choose to be listed—of moms, grouped by state and city, who are willing to be called in emergencies. Think of it as a national phone directory of helpers for your cadet. It can also serve as a resource for you if you need a point of contact while traveling. It really is like having an adoptive family all across the country.

CHAPTER 31
Bragging Right
(avoiding resentment)

Unless your cadet is an only child (with no relatives), resentment is likely to rear its ugly head some time during the 47-month West Point experience. In a perfect world, everyone would be happy for the times your cadet meets sitting presidents, beauty queens, and Chuck Norris. They would be thrilled to hear tales of traveling the globe on the government's nickel, dining with ambassadors (oh, wait, that was my son), and ringing the bell to open the stock exchange. And yes, there's a top-notch education in there as well. This is all good news that you would expect to be able to celebrate freely with friends and family.

Alas, this is not the case. Eventually, even your best friends will tire of hearing what a great experience your cadet is having. If your friends don't want to hear about it, try to imagine how weary your other children (who are usually achieving some pretty amazing things of their own) might become, since they hear more than anyone about their sibling's successes and adventures. One mom's son unfriended her from Facebook so he didn't have to read any more updates about his brother! Remember to celebrate the accomplishments of all your children. If you are fortunate enough to have your cadet's grandparents still with you, you may find they are just about the only ones who never tire of hearing cadet success/brag stories.

As women, we are talkers. We want to share with others about our lives and our kids. Where are you going to go when your friends are sick of West Point? This is where the amazing network called "West Point Moms" comes in. Once you plug in with the moms (whether online or through a Parents' Club), you have a network of friends who totally "get it." The West Point Moms want to know when your cadet accomplishes something great. We celebrate the victories, both big and small, with each other. This isn't to say the Moms are perfect; we also can get snarky, especially when we see amazing experiences our cadets didn't get to take advantage of; however, the West Point experience is what our cadets make it. Whether it's success in academics, sports, leadership, or other accomplishments, it's all there for our cadets. You've got a lot to brag about. Tell the Moms—we want to hear!

CHAPTER 32

Get Involved
(opportunities to be active with other parents)

Women—we're such social creatures! I think we need each other. As a new mom, I needed other women to help me know what to do, encourage me when I was down and motivate me to keep going on my worst days. So it is with the West Point Mom experience. Fortunately for those moms who need to be around others, there are plenty of opportunities!

For most West Point Moms, the local Parents' Club is the first POC (so you don't have to check the "Lingo" chapter, it means "Point of Contact"). If your Parents' Club hasn't been in touch with you by R-Day, you can initiate contact—if not in the Eisenhower ballroom, then online later. The West Point Parent Liaison keeps a list of active Parents' Clubs and will have a link to your Parents' Club posted online. You can find this information on the West Point website (www.usma.edu/parents). Clubs meet periodically for socials and cadet support activities.

Some clubs are very active, hosting events such as West

Point football game tailgates, while others (generally closer to New York) sponsor buses to transport cadets for holidays. Some clubs, like the one in Georgia, meet twice a year to pack boodle for every cadet from that state. This sounds like quite an undertaking until you see that the club for Northern Virginia, District of Columbia, and Maryland packs boodle for the entire Corps of Cadets!

Wouldn't a more experienced West Point Mom be a helpful companion on this journey? Some clubs have mentor programs in which parents of upperclassmen help Plebe parents through the first year. For parents with no military experience, these relationships can be very helpful. If your club doesn't offer this, ask for it—many parents are willing to help, if you only ask.

In many states, Cadet Candidates are invited to a Founder's Day banquet to celebrate the founding of West Point. Attending this event provides an opportunity to meet other parents in the local club. These contacts can prove to be lifelines as you navigate the West Point journey. You will have questions as a West Point Mom. Books and social networks are good, but real, face-to-face people are even better.

In Atlanta, as well as in some other larger cities, the Army and Navy parents get together each year at a local sports bar to watch The Big Game. For those who do not travel to see the Army-Navy (football) game in person, this is a fun alternative—also, it's warmer than sitting in the stands in December! Again, check with your Parents' Club to see what they have scheduled. If they've never scheduled a viewing party, maybe your contribution to the club will be to set one up!

Within the clubs are numerous opportunities to get

involved. Parents are needed to fill both officer and committee positions. Parents plan larger cadet support events such as a yearly send-off picnic where recent graduates are honored and incoming Cadet Candidates are recognized. Along with Parents' Clubs from the other service academies, parents organize an All-Academy Ball (a formal event for all cadets in the five service academies). If your club sponsors a tailgate at a West Point home game (or an away game in your area), you could help with organizing that. Some clubs are simply a social place for parents in the area to gather and talk about their cadets. It's kind of nice to be in a room full of people who actually ask you to brag about your cadet.

West Point Moms are always looking for ways to get involved. Moms are used to doing for others, and taking care of cadets is just another way to do this. If a sports team is coming to your town, you could organize a dinner or send goodies to the team. One year when the divers trained in Knoxville on winter break, some wonderful Tennessee Parents' Club members hosted a Southern barbeque (with sweet tea, of course). You will find that Parents' Clubs enjoy treating all cadets as if they were their own. If you hear that cadets are traveling to your area, consider reaching out to them to see how you or your club can support them.

Some of the West Point Moms who met online in our Facebook group (www.facebook/WestPointMoms) started a troop support organization called West Point Moms Bake (www.facebook/WestPointMomsBake). Each month, the moms send boxes of homemade goodies to troops serving in Afghanistan. The moms have bonded over the activity and love sharing the thank-you notes that come from the recipients. In a few years, it might be other West Point Moms doing this for our sons and daughters. Sometimes it's the little things we can reach out and do that make the biggest differences in someone's life. The moms in the baking group have built relationships with each other (although most have never met in person) as they've worked toward the common goal of troop support.

What if you really want to get involved, but you live in a rural area or an area so remote that you have no club within a reasonable distance? This is all the more reason to connect trough technology. Do not wait until you are lonely, overwhelmed, and staring out that window, wondering if there is a mom remotely close to you and understanding your need. Quick! Run to your computer and start connecting! You do not have to feel isolated. The wonders of technology now connect West Point parents so that everyone can be just as involved as those in major metropolitan areas.

Whether providing food, welcoming troops at the local USO, or volunteering at the myriad of military events in your area, your first place to get this information is your local (even if distant) Parents' Club. Getting involved is a small way we parents can give back and stay busy while we miss our kids.

CHAPTER 33

Support Your Local Academy
(fundraising for USMA)

Contrary to what some may believe, West Point is not fully funded by the United States government. Roughly 10% of the funding for West Point comes from private support. One group or another is always more than happy to accept your tax-deductible donation. Trying to figure out where your donated dollar ends up can be frustrating. The following is a brief explanation of the money trail.

First of all, the United States Military Academy is prohibited from soliciting funds because Federal law doesn't allow military personnel or representatives of the Federal government to do so. Therefore, the West Point Association of Graduates (WPAOG) functions as the fundraising arm for the Academy. Though its name sounds like an alumni club, WPAOG exists for the sole purpose of benefiting the Corps of Cadets and the Academy.

The WPAOG funds "Margin of Excellence" programs, which complement the Academy's programs in admissions, academics, activities, athletics, leadership education, and other opportunities for cadets. Parents can give to WPAOG through an unrestricted annual fund called the West Point Parents' Fund, or they can choose to designate to a specific program. The fundraising for WPAOG is done through mail solicitations and a phone-a-thon. You will be contacted with a suggested donation amount. Obviously parents can give whatever they choose (or not at all). Just know that you will be contacted.

The Directorate of Cadet Activities (DCA) receives some of the funds raised by WPAOG. DCA oversees all co-curricular clubs, Ike Hall performances, and social events for the cadets. Parents contributing to DCA can designate their donation to a specific club or team (e.g, Powerlifting Team, Fly Fishing Club, Gospel Choir).

Gifts to WPAOG may be directed to the Army A Club to support Corps squad teams. Unrestricted gifts to the A Club support all Corps squad athletes and also qualify donors for certain annual benefits (including season football tickets, special parking passes, and the right to buy Army-Navy tickets), dependent upon the level of the gift. Donors can also choose to restrict their donations to specific teams via the "Friends of" program to supplement individual team budgets. For example, the Swimming and Diving Team has an annual fundraiser sponsored by a group called Friends of Army Swimming and Diving. Giving directly to a team is just another option for your donation dollars; however, "Friends of" gifts do not qualify donors for any annual benefits associated with the A Club.

Another non-profit group that may contact you for a donation is called West-Point.org. West-Point.org connects parents, graduates, and friends of USMA by means of a website and several e-mail groups such as prospect-net, plebe-net, parent-net, and others. It is important to note that this organization is not officially tied to the Academy. Thus, their fundraisers keep their website and e-mail lists going but do not directly fund the Academy or cadets.

When you are ready to part with your donation dollars, rest assured you will have plenty of options! Hopefully this chapter has helped you understand a little more about the choices you have for directing your generosity. For further information, please check the website www.westpointaog.org.

CHAPTER 34
The Chain
(understanding the Chain of Command)

In the olden days, the chain of command was simple: we told our kids what to do, and they did it. Now as West Point cadets, our kids have an entire structure in place for determining who tells them what to do, how to do it, and when to do it. Those not from a military background often have questions about how the whole West Point Chain of Command functions, so I'm including a brief overview.

The Corps of Cadets is comprised of 4,400 men and women. They are organized into 36 cadet companies, which are grouped into battalions of three companies each. The battalions are grouped into regiments (three battalions per regiment). Four regiments make up the brigade, also known as the United States Corps of Cadets.

Whew! It's a lot to take in, but your cadet will be instructed over and over in "the Chain." In the past, some kids relied on parents to solve their dilemmas; now, they have the Chain. Let's start at the top of the cadet Chain and see how it trickles down.

Cadets run the Corps through their Chain of Command.

The top-ranking First Class cadet (Firstie) is in the role of First Captain, whose role is Brigade Commander. Firsties are also Regimental Commanders, Battalion Commanders, Company Commanders, and Platoon Leaders. Primary staff roles at brigade, regiment, battalion, company, and platoon levels are filled by Firsties, and Brigade and Regimental Sergeants Major are also Firsties.

Reporting to all these commanders and staff officers are Second Class cadets (Cows) who serve as Squad Leaders, Sergeants Major (at battalion level), First Sergeants, Platoon Sergeants and staff NCOs (Noncommissioned Officers). Additionally, Firsties can have assistants who are Cows on staff at all levels.

Third Class cadets (Yearlings or Yuks) are next down the Chain as Team Leaders. They oversee one or two Fourth Class cadets at the bottom of the Chain.

A team is made up of a Team Leader and Plebe(s). A squad is made up of two or three teams. Four squads make up a platoon. Four platoons make up a company.

But wait! That's not all. There are full-time professional military officers in charge of the Corps of Cadets, linking the Chain to the regular Army. The highest-ranking officer on post is the Superintendent, and just below him is the Commandant of Cadets. Both are Army generals. Next, the Brigade Tactical Officer, a Colonel, heads up the Brigade Tactical Department, which is in charge of all military training for the Corps of Cadets. This department is staffed by active duty military officers who work directly with the cadet Chain of Command. Each Regiment is led by a Regimental Tactical Officer who is a Lieutenant Colonel. A Major or Captain serves in each cadet company as a Company Tactical

Officer (TAC), assisted by a Master Sergeant or Sergeant First Class who is the Company Tactical Noncommissioned Officer (TAC NCO).

The TACs and TAC NCOs oversee each cadet's development while at West Point. Each one acts as teacher, leader, mentor, role model, and administrator for roughly one hundred cadets and is ultimately responsible for doing everything possible to ensure your cadet's success at West Point.

Why does any of this matter to a West Point Mom? Sometimes we like to get involved and help our cadets figure out a situation or problem. It's our nature to go "straight to the top." It's important, though, for us to understand that at West Point there is a process of accountability and leadership in place, and going to the person at the top is not the way to handle most issues. We must bear this in mind when listening to complaints from our cadets. Sometimes they just want to gripe a bit to us, but in order to solve the problem they know they must go through the Chain. They are not looking for us to play the role of "Mommy the Fixer."

The system works. Understanding the Chain of Command helps us see why a situation might take a little longer to resolve than any of us would like. Navigating through the process is the way our cadets have to deal with situations at West Point. Understanding the process helps us support our cadets.

CHAPTER 35
Life Lessons
(what West Point Moms have learned in 47 months or less)

Whath's the point of the journey if you don't learn anything? Surely it's not just the thrill of the ride. As we come to the close of our own 47-month West Point adventures, we look back on how much our sons have grown and how much we've changed as moms and as women. We've chosen to conclude our book with some words of wisdom from moms who are themselves West Point survivors. Here are some of the things these West Point Moms have learned in 47 months or less.

- Everything really is going to be okay, and that doesn't necessarily mean that everything will go according to plan. It's not a smooth road and not every cadet follows it to its end, but that's okay, too.

- I do not have to be so involved, I do not have to buy the T-shirt, and it does not make me a bad mother if my experience is different.

- If things don't bother my cadet, they should not bother me.

- Success comes from all walks of life, all levels of wealth or poverty, all social levels, etc.; if we judge based on any criteria other than one's merit, we are doing everyone a disservice.

- I can't force my daughter to like something or do something, but she does listen to me even when I don't think she can hear any reason.

- Don't give advice or an opinion unless specifically asked for it. Cadets have enough people around them who are able to give them good advice, and enough people who are adding to their stress, without my doing it. My job now is to support, encourage, love and provide a safe place to vent and complain.

- "Patriotism" now has an inexplicable meaning to me as my child not only understands, but accepts, that service means she will risk life and limb for her country. That has changed me in ways I have yet to fully define.

- "Hold on loosely, but don't let go" (in the words of the 38 Special song from my rockin' '80's youth!)

- Make him laugh and we all have a good week.

- My worrying is more about me and less about my cadet, so I try not to burden him with my worrying because it's not really productive and doesn't help him.

- There are different kinds of pride. I am more proud of my son than I can say. But I was proud of him before West Point; this is the icing on the cake.

- He is in the Army now. In other words, it isn't my job to fill out paperwork, find answers, help with homework, or make life easier for him. It is my job to encourage him to do all of that for himself, to keep the end in mind, and to pray!

- West Point has put a lot of money and effort into our cadets and does not want to see them fail. I have to have faith in that, and I need to pass that on to my cadet.

- Plan everything to the minute years ahead and remain flexible enough to change everything at the very last second.

- Having a child at West Point is good for my prayer life.

- Even though you think your children aren't listening to you, they most certainly are. I like the respectful cadet who values his parents' opinions even when they are different from his own.

- Kids grow up, and sometimes not exactly the way you had hoped, but if you can let go of that, you will see that it's usually not a bad thing.

- Do not alter anything in her home bedroom without permission!

- Learn to step back and let him make the choices that are right for him. Cut apron strings and let him fly. He knows we are here for him, but he is an adult now and needs to be treated as such.

- The desire to serve comes from within. West Point has and needs all types; cadets from the dyed-in-the-wool military families to the die-hard pacifist families, cadets who grew up outspoken and confident to those who quietly succeed. It is this broad range of cadets who will give our military the fine character and adaptability required in today's world.

- Uniforms seem to hold onto smells. Don't wash stinky Soldier laundry in Lysol, though. If you do, you will re-wash that load six times to get the Lysol smell out!

- Don't pack plastic fruit cups next to hard pointy things in a boodle box.

- Maturity comes a lot more quickly at West Point than it would with a more traditional college experience.

- Don't whine so much! Have more of a "can-do" attitude. (A few times when I have talked to my cadet about something going on in my life, his response has been, "So what are you going to do?" or "Make it happen!")

- Buy tissue; buy stock in tissue.

- Don't be all "Go Army" if you have other children. They are just as important and noble as the cadet, just following a different route. Promote them, too!

- Checking all the pockets in the cadet's duffle bag when he throws it downstairs to the laundry room is not a good idea. There are some things you may not want to know.

- I like my Plebe son a whole lot more now than I did when he was a high school kid… he's more respectful and responsible. We've taken our complicated mother-son relationship to a whole new level. Dare I say we are getting very close to an adult-adult relationship!

- Plebes, in general, are miserable, so don't ask if he

likes it there, or if it now feels like home.

- You are not a horrible mom if you hold the phone out at arm's length while he rants, and occasionally pull it back to your mouth enough to mumble an "I'm so sorry," "mmmm," and "awwww."

- Even college seniors (and yes, even top-of-the-Chain Firsties) get homesick.

- Don't try to make everything easier for him or to lighten his load by doing things like taxes, passport, airline tickets, etc., for him.

- Being an Army wife is way easier than being an Army mom. Watching my husband parade has always filled me with pride but never brought me to tears; not so for my son.

- Let go of worrying about grades and class standing. Cadets know what it means (the better they do, the more options they have), and our adding to their stress does not really help them—it just adds to their stress. Instead of trying to give guidance, which they do not need so much, give them support and love… and sympathy.

- It's okay to slip and be a helicopter mom once in a while; I've raised a great kid and he will forgive me for it—as long as I don't abuse it.

- This is my cadet's journey, and he must make it on his own. But the strength of his hug when we meet lets me know I'm still a big part of his life. Unconditional love is what he needs now.

- Listen more, speak less, and pray harder.

- Learn to let go. My dreams for him are not his dreams. Once I accepted that, I found peace, and I have nothing but pride for him.

Finally, there is one lesson we all learned in grade school that still applies: there is safety in numbers. This is a new journey for your cadet. It's also a new journey for you. Surround yourself with people who have been there, people who know the way and can encourage you. The West Point Moms are here to help.

.

LINGO

(a glossary of acronyms and
terms common to West Point)

LINGO

(a glossary of acronyms and terms common to West Point)

There is a whole vocabulary that goes with every new activity, but the military seems to pride itself on making that vocabulary exquisitely obscure. We think there must be a staff position somewhere with the specific duty assignment of researching the least direct way of saying something, then making a TLA (Three-Letter Acronym) for it. That would be the LOO—the Language Obfuscation Officer. We imagine the LOO would be the person responsible for re-naming a test in an academic class as a "Written Partial Review" (WPR) and a final (you know, the last test of the term, at a civilian school) as a "Term End Examination" (TEE).

So, how's a mom to learn all the letters and their meanings? Just do your best and crank up that sense of humor. You're not going to get them all right, maybe ever— maybe your cadet won't either! But give it a try, because it gives you a link to the cadet's world. Laugh at yourself; laugh with your cadet as he or she laughs at you; laugh at the whole process.

We've put together a list of acronyms and other lingo that you'll be expected to master before you're allowed to take a seat at Michie (see below) for graduation. (Don't panic; we're kidding.) You might just want to use this for reference, rather than trying to memorize it outright. Maybe get it temporarily tattooed on your forearm or at least posted somewhere near the phone you use when talking to your cadet. Use your knowledge with caution, though. Sometimes cadets don't want you actually to *speak* their language.

Here goes!

100th Night

roughly 100 nights before graduation, this is a winter banquet and celebration for Firsties

2LT

Second Lieutenant, the rank your cadet will receive upon commissioning into the Army, immediately following graduation

500th Night

about 500 nights before graduation, this is the Cows' celebration banquet

ACU

Army Combat Uniform; the tan and gray digitally camouflaged ones (as of 2012, these will be changing, and there will be a new acronym with the new clothes)

A-Day

Acceptance Day, in late August; the day New Cadets are officially received into the Corps of Cadets as Plebes; rank changes from New Cadet to Cadet on this day

AI

Additional Instruction; this is generally time spent with a professor to get help with an academic subject

AOG

See WPAOG

APFT

Army Physical Fitness Test; this changes from time to time, but currently includes standards for running, sit-ups and push-ups

AY

Academic Year, the time from beginning of fall semester to end of spring semester each year

Barracks

the buildings where cadets are housed; NOT dormitories; dorms are for civilians

BCG

Birth Control Glasses/Goggles; officially designated as TEDs, these are the glasses issued for use during Beast Barracks, and they are singularly unfashionable, thus ensuring that the wearer will not be sexually active

Beast or, more formally, **Beast Barracks**

the nickname for Cadet Basic Training, the first few intense weeks at West Point

Boodle

snacks, sweets, and other treats sent to cadets; only a certain quantity may be stored in their rooms, in a boodle box which fits on a specific shelf in the barracks closet

Branch Night

in the fall of Firstie year, the night when cadets are assigned to the various branches of military service; there is some choice in this assignment, based on class rank and whatever system the Academy chooses to use to make the assignments

Buckner

Camp Buckner, a training area at West Point; site of the field training during CBT and CFT

Butt

usually "and a butt"; a partial remaining portion (like a cigarette butt); example of use: "three weeks and a butt" means "three weeks and an unspecified number of days"

Cadet Candidate

official designation of one who has accepted the appointment to USMA but has not yet been received into training

Cadre

the leadership team in a training program

CBT

Cadet Basic Training; first summer at USMA, also referred to as "Beast"; basic military and leadership training

CFT

Cadet Field Training; second summer at USMA, more basic military and leadership training; sometimes this is called "Buckner" because it takes place almost completely at Camp Buckner

Chain of Command
the people in authority over your cadet; the number of people in the Chain and their titles will vary depending on your cadet's rank and position

CLDT
Cadet Leader Development Training; required field training held at Camp Buckner

CO
Commanding Officer; cadet head of a company

Com
see "Commandant"

Combatives
physical combat training required of all cadets prior to graduation; female cadets take this instead of Plebe boxing

Commandant
Commandant of Cadets; the Army General in charge of military development of the Corps

COR
Cadet Observation Report; may be positive or negative; a report on a cadet by any other person

Corps of Cadets (the Corps)
the West Point equivalent of "the student body"; the group of cadets currently attending West Point

Corps squad
a team representing the Academy in NCAA intercollegiate competition

Cow

third year at West Point (like junior year at other colleges)

Cow Commitment

formally called the Affirmation Ceremony; at the beginning of Cow year, the time when cadets formalize their commitment by making a contract to serve in the Army five years on active duty and three years in the reserves; in general, if a cadet leaves West Point after Commitment, service in the Army is still required

CPRC

Cadet Public Relations Council; an opportunity provided to cadets through the Admissions office to speak in their home communities about USMA; for those chosen it means a few days extra leave before a holiday break

CTLT

Cadet Troop Leader Training; required on-the-job training, shadowing a Lieutenant and possibly acting as a Second Lieutenant in a position at an active Army post

DAC

Department Academic Counselor; faculty member who assists cadets in choosing classes in the later years when they actually get to make such choices

DCA

Directorate of Cadet Activities; department of the Academy responsible for coordinating "entertainment, extracurricular, recreational, cultural and social activities" (from the website, www.allforthecorps.com) and producing various publications such as yearbooks and calendars

Dean

Dean of the Academy Board; as in a civilian school, the Dean oversees the academic life of the Corps

Firstie

senior or last year at West Point; the name is left from the old system of referring to each class with a number, beginning with Fourth Class cadets and working upward each year until reaching First Class

Firstie Club

"The First Class Club," a bar on campus for Firsties only

Hop

a dance

Hours

time spent walking back and forth under the supervision of a cadet member of Chain of Command; earned as punishment for any number of infractions

HUA

Pronounced "Hooah." Heard. Understood. Acknowledged.

IAD

Individual Advanced Development, which can be Academic (AIAD), Military (MIAD), or Physical (PIAD); similar to an internship; not a required program, but an option some cadets will pursue

Ice Cream Social

a gathering during Beast Barracks at the home of a family stationed at West Point where New Cadets have access to electronic communication, a bit of freedom, and some ice cream as well

Ike or **Ike Hall**

Eisenhower Hall, where R-Day activities begin and many other events are held; "Ike" was a nickname for President Dwight D. Eisenhower (USMA 1915), for whom the building is named

Land Nav

Land Navigation; finding one's way through the field or forest or swamp or desert (in day or night, rain or shine) using various maps and navigation tools

Long Gray Line

all graduates of the United States Military Academy; the Line goes back over 200 years to 1802

March Back

a 12.5-mile march from Camp Buckner to the USMA campus at the end of Beast; the New Cadets are often joined by graduates, including members of the USMA class fifty years ahead of them (1962 joined the 2012 class, for example)

Michie

pronounced "MIKE-ee"; Michie Stadium, site of the football games your cadet is required to attend unless other duties preclude attendance

Million-Dollar View

a view of the Hudson from near Trophy Point

MRE

Meal Ready to Eat; common food for cadets out in field training; these don't require cooking and they are designed to provide balanced nutrition for survival (not necessarily for pleasure)

NC

New Cadet; this title is earned on R-Day and held until A-Day

OPP

Off-Post Privileges; permission to go beyond the gates, usually within a 70- to 75-mile distance of post

Order of merit

class rank, which includes academic, physical, and military performance scores

PDA

Public Display of Affection; physical contact between members of opposing genders while on post or in uniform, restricted to certain specific behaviors; moms, however, are always entitled to hugs

Plain, The

Not being grads ourselves, we are not fully qualified to describe this significant piece of real estate, but for the uninitiated, it is a parade ground, and no one but members of the Corps of Cadets or the Long Gray Line must tread there.

Plebe

first year at West Point; think "Plebeian," as in human being with no rights and lots of duties

PMI

Afternoon (P.M.) Inspection of cadet barracks; these can be required at any time, but one of the most frequently awarded privileges is a PMI card, which excuses a cadet from PMI and gives permission to close the door to the cadet's room and even to take a nap during that period of time

Post

the land surrounding the campus of USMA; West Point is not only the location of the Academy, but it is also the oldest continually active military base (post) on U.S. soil; on-post means within the gates of West Point and off-post means outside the gates

POV

Privately Owned Vehicle (replaces commonly used CAR)

PPW

Plebe Parent Weekend; a long weekend of activities at USMA to give parents and families of Plebes a chance to glimpse the cadet's world, meet professors, dine in the dining hall, visit the barracks, and dance the night away

PX

Post Exchange, a department store on-post for military personnel; military ID is required to purchase items there; there is a PX at West Point which is a good source for boodle boxes, boots and shoes, among other things

QPA

Quality Point Average (sort of a weighted Grade Point Average)

Quality Points

Points earned based on letter grade in an academic course, on a four-point scale where an A is 4 points, but fractional points are awarded as well (for example, C- is 1.67; C is 2.00; C+ is 2.33)

R-Day

Reception Day, the day Cadet Candidates report to USMA and become New Cadets

Reorgy

Reorganization, a time at the beginning of each academic semester during which company positions, personal duties, room assignments, and roommates are changed

Review

parade; cadets march in formation for review by visiting dignitaries (as well as parents and other spectators)

Ring Poop

a recitation of fawning praise for the class rings just awarded to Firsties on Ring Weekend; this is one of the few times Plebes are allowed to speak to upperclassmen without being addressed first, so they run down the Firsties to recite the lines; see www.youtube.com for video

Ring Weekend

near the beginning of fall semester, a celebration centered on the receiving of class rings; cadets order rings in winter of Cow year and receive them at the start of Firstie year

SAMI

Saturday morning (A.M.) Inspection; this is a white-glove inspection where everything in a cadet's barracks room has to be in place, dusted, polished, and/or scrubbed; cadets sometimes stay up most of Friday night getting ready for a SAMI

Sandhurst

named after the British Royal Military Academy Sandhurst, this is a competition among teams from military academies around the world; it is a timed obstacle course with various challenges of strength, endurance, orienteering and speed; each West Point cadet company has a team, and each team must have one female member

Separation

the process of leaving the Academy prior to graduation, as required by the Academy, due to a cadet's failure to meet physical, military, academic or ethical standards

Sponsor

a member of military who offers to help a cadet adjust to being in a new locale; sponsors invite cadets into their homes and may offer help in the form of rides, directions, or other counsel as cadets get accustomed to the Academy; this program is offered at military bases around the world to help new assignees adjust to their new posts

STAP

Summer Term Academic Program; summer school, offered in some cases, either for remedial or for supplemental or accelerated study, but enrollment is dependent on the timing of a cadet's summer military training

Supe or **Superintendent**

Superintendent, United States Military Academy; the highest ranking officer on post at West Point and an Army General; the Commandant of Cadets, Dean of the

Academic Board, and several other officers report directly to the Supe

TAC

Tactical Officer; active duty military officer responsible for a Cadet Company; this person approves all leaves and passes and is in the information loop for all reports on a cadet's standing in academic, military, and physical development

TAC NCO

Tactical Non-Commissioned Officer; active duty enlisted service member who advises and assists cadets in military, academic and personal development

TED

Tactical Eye Device; these are the glasses issued when cadets arrive on R-Day, for them to use instead of their own glasses during Beast; they are not especially attractive, giving rise to their nickname, BCG

TEE

Term End Examination; final exam in an academic class

Thayer Week

a week when a cadet has several tests, papers, and/ or projects due; named for Colonel Sylvanus Thayer, Superintendent of USMA from 1817 to 1833, who developed the academic system still used at the Academy today, emphasizing self-study, daily homework, and small class size

TL

Team Leader; in cadet terms, this is the job of a Yuk who is responsible for one or two Plebes; together they form a team; the Team Leader is tasked with aiding in the academic, military, physical, and moral development of the Plebes on the team

Transient Barracks

residence for cadets in transition for medical or administrative reasons; recovery from injury or non-contagious illness, considering resignation from the Academy, and separation are all reasons for housing here

Trophy Point

an area directly overlooking the Hudson River with an assortment of war trophies (captured artillery pieces) and a 46-foot-tall granite column, a monument to Civil War veterans; easy to spot, it is a campus landmark and meeting place

Waldo

based on the *Where's Waldo?* hidden picture books, this nickname highlights the difficulty of spotting a particular cadet in the sea of similarly coiffed and costumed young folks; finding one's own Waldo in pictures posted online becomes a favorite parental pastime during Beast summer

Walking Privileges

permission to leave post but remain within "walking distance" of the gates; the perimeter of walking privileges at a given time is specifically known to cadets, and they will also be advised of hours and uniform requirements that must be observed

WAMI

Wednesday morning (A.M.) Inspection; see "SAMI"

WPAOG

Association of Graduates; a very involved and supportive alumni association, most of whose efforts go toward supporting cadets

WPR

Written Partial Review; a test

Yearling or **Yuk**

sophomore or second year at West Point

YWW

Yearling Winter Weekend—the celebration weekend for second-year students, with a banquet and a hop

Please note that this is far from an exhaustive list. The LOO is working on this full-time, after all, so new abbreviations are probably coming out even as you read this. OK, really, there's no LOO, but the military is very good at naming and abbreviating things in ways that seem strange to us outsiders, and even to some insiders. Use this list as a beginning guide, and add to your own TLA vocabulary as you're able.

CPSIA information can be obtained at www.ICGtesting.com
Printed in the USA
LVOW111235110612

285575LV00002B/3/P